D1453175

AMITYVILLE PUBLIC LIBRARY

The Ransom of the Jews

The Ransom
of the Jews

*The Story of the
Extraordinary Secret Bargain
Between Romania and Israel*

RADU IOANID

*With a Foreword by Elie Wiesel
and an Afterword by Ion Pacepa*

IVAN R. DEE
Chicago 2005

THE RANSOM OF THE JEWS. Copyright © 2005 by Radu Ioanid.
All rights reserved, including the right to reproduce this book or
portions thereof in any form. For information, address: Ivan R. Dee,
Publisher, 1332 North Halsted Street, Chicago 60622. Manufactured in
the United States and printed on acid-free paper.

Library of Congress Cataloging-in-Publication Data:
Ioanid, Radu.
    The ransom of the Jews : the story of the extraordinary secret
bargain between Romania and Israel / Radu Ioanid.
        p. cm.
    Includes bibliographical references and index.
    ISBN 1-56663-562-4 (alk. paper)
        1. Jews—Romania—History—20th century. 2. Romania—
Emigration and immigration. 3. Israel—Emigration and immigration.
4. Romania—Emigration and immigration—Government policy. 5.
Ransom—Romania—History—20th century. 6. Romania—History—
1944–1989. I. Title.

DS135.R7I66 2005
323.1192'40498'09045—dc22

                                                    2004056103

In memory of my father, Virgil, who used to tell me that the Communist regime of Romania succeeded where both the Iron Guards and Ion Antonescu had failed—in making Romania a country free of Jews.

Acknowledgments

THE IDEA FOR THIS BOOK belongs to David Singer, director of research at the American Jewish Committee. It
was he who first proposed that I undertake this compelling
and challenging research, and the AJC initially sponsored
my efforts. Thanks to the dedicated support of this organization and of the United States Congress, I was able to gain
access to highly classified Romanian official records in the
archives of several intelligence agencies. The AJC also graciously agreed to permit me to transform my research report into a book. Thus I am grateful to the organization in
general and specifically to David Singer, Andrew Baker, and
David Harris.

Both in Romania and in Israel, my research on this sensitive piece of history raised eyebrows among certain bureaucrats with little understanding of history. They feared the
skeletons in the closets of their governments. Despite this attitude, I was able to find in government circles of both countries wonderful friends who helped make this book possible.

In Romania, President Emil Constantinescu and some
of his advisers supported my work wholeheartedly. I am

grateful to Professor Zoe Petre, the president's chief of staff, and to Marius Oprea, adviser to the president, for their warm assistance. Both understood immediately the ethical and moral implications of my work and backed it without hesitation. The successive leaderships (under Presidents Constantinescu and Iliescu) of the Romanian Information Service (SRI) declassified and made available to me a great many documents which were crucial to an understanding of the surveillance and repression of the Romanian Jewish community by the Communist secret police, the feared Securitate. I want to thank especially Costin Georgescu and Radu Timofte, directors of SRI, and General Marius Brateanu, the SRI's general secretary, for their efficient help.

The Romanian Ministry of Foreign Affairs, through Mircea Geoana, Romanian ambassador to Washington, and Dumitru Preda, director of the ministry's archives, helped me find documents that contributed greatly to an understanding of the complex history that I relate in this book.

I am grateful to Dan Badea, a gifted journalist, and to Cornel Burtica, a former Communist leader who willingly left the party leadership. Both enabled me to understand the direct connection between Nicolae Ceausescu and the trade in human beings.

In Romania I was permitted access to highly classified documents that officially do not exist. I have had to refer to them in the following pages as "documents from a Romanian government archive that requested anonymity." Those people who kindly and efficiently helped me see these records understand why I cannot mention their names here.

In Israel, Shlomo Leibovici-Lais, formerly with the Liaison Bureau, guided me through the complicated institutional history of the *alyah* of Romanian Jews to Israel. His humor, wisdom, and deep knowledge of both Israeli and Romanian history were essential in helping me compose this book. He allowed me to understand a key fact about the Romanian trade in human beings—that there was more to this trade than simply a matter of finances. The archivist of the state of Israel, Tuvia Friling, made available to me important declassified documents in English and Hebrew; with his newly published book, which I had the privilege to consult in manuscript, they shed new light on Ben-Gurion's role during World War II and on the emigration of Romanian Jews to Israel. I am also grateful to Tuvia for putting me in touch with Ephraim Illin, one of the lesser-known heroes of Israel who helped me clarify the financial history of the Romanian Jewish emigration.

A group of distinguished Israeli diplomats offered advice and comment. I am grateful to Ambassador Meir Rosenne, former legal adviser to Prime Minister Menachem Begin at Camp David, specifically for his insights on the late Chief Rabbi Moses Rosen. My thanks to Ambassador Yosef Govrin for his comments and subtle analysis of Israeli-Romanian relations during the last years of the Ceausescu regime. Because of Ambassador Govrin, I was better able to understand the human rights dimension of Israeli foreign policy during those years. I also appreciate the wise comments of Ambassador Abba Gefen. The late Yitzhak Artzi, formerly deputy mayor of Tel Aviv and member of the Knesset, gave me interesting leads and documents. May he rest in peace.

In Great Britain, Phyllis Yadin helped me understand Henry Jacober's role. In the United States, General Ion

Mihai Pacepa, former deputy head of Romanian foreign intelligence and the highest-ranking defector in the history of the cold war, condemned twice to death by Ceausescu for his defection, spent many hours of his time guiding me through the organization and history of the Securitate and its trade in human beings. I am grateful to him for his unwavering support. Liviu Turcu, former head of the Western European and later the North American department of Romanian foreign intelligence, who defected to the United States early in 1989 and was also condemned to death in Romania, guided me through the Securitate's complicated financial operations.

Nestor Rates, for many years director of the Romanian department of Radio Free Europe, provided me with crucial details. Robert Levy graciously provided me with many useful documents originating from the Romanian Communist party archives. Mircea Raceanu, former head of the North American desk in the Romanian Ministry of Foreign Affairs, once imprisoned and condemned to death by Ceausescu, patiently explained to me the almost total control of that ministry by the Securitate. Ambassador Alfred Moses shared with me his impressions about his meetings with Ceausescu. I am grateful to them all for their patient support.

My friends and colleagues Paul Shapiro and Daniel Mariaschin helped me understand the dilemmas that confronted Washington in its foreign policy decisions regarding Romania during the Ceausescu regime.

I owe a special thanks to Elie Wiesel, who strongly encouraged me to write this book and, when I felt discouraged, insisted that the truth is ultimately more important than the adverse reactions of various bureaucracies. Finally,

I am exceedingly grateful to my publisher and editor, Ivan Dee, who patiently persevered with the preparation of my manuscript. His help and understanding have made this book possible.

R. I.

Washington, D.C.
September 2004

Contents

Foreword

A Letter to the Author from Elie Wiesel

DEAR RADU,

I have just finished reading your book. How to describe it? This story is sober and troubling—the historical analysis striking, the investigation documented with hidden and painful truths: it is all of this and even more. Anyone who is interested in the events that will forever mark the destiny of a people and their thirst for humanity—I speak of course about what is so poorly, in the absence of truer words, called the Holocaust—must read it. This is true also in terms of Jewish community life in the 1950s, '60s, and '70s. The atmosphere of fear and distrust, the role of American Jews, and Rabbi Rosen and his (too close?) relationship with the Romanian government, his courageous fight against anti-Semitism, his contribution to the massive emigration of so many Jews to Israel—you speak of these matters with eloquence and discretion. You do not judge, you only observe and record the story.

Born like you, but before you, in Romania, I thought I knew everything about the fate of the Jews during the war and later under the Communist regime. The violent and brutal anti-Semitism of the Iron Guard, the fascist policies of Ion Antonescu, the savage pogroms and deportations of thousands and thousands of Jewish families to Transnistria where they would suffer and perish—I knew about these things vaguely enough. But I did not know about the historical context of the official and "respectable" hatred that permeated all aspects of daily life—all vile, narrow-minded, and stupid. I did not know, for example, that at the beginning of the 1940s Romanian Jews were able to buy bread at a high price—but not pastry. And that laws as aberrant and humiliating as the numerus clausus—the quota system— affected the Jewish deaf and dumb too: they were excluded from their own association. As were doctors, journalists, teachers, and architects. Just as in the time of the Romans after the destruction of the Temple of Jerusalem, an official decree of 1940 forbade the Jews the right to be students and teachers.

I learned much about the complex relations between Romania and Israel. Golda Meir escaped an Arab attempt on her life, at the entrance to the main synagogue in the Romanian capital, thanks to the Securitate. . . . Ceausescu served as the middleman between Menachem Begin and Anwar el Sadat in order to conclude the peace between Israel and Egypt. . . . All of this you relate based upon information from apparently trustworthy sources.

But your real revelations concern the transformation of the Romanian government into an extraordinary merchant of human beings during the postwar years. Here and there rumors circulated about this. If 380,000 Romanian Jews established themselves in the Jewish State, it is because Romania "sold" them as if they were slaves. In other words, certain Romanian Jews were able to obtain visas to go abroad, especially to Israel, in return for payments in dollars. You provide names and figures. Am I surprised? No. I do remember that in the little villages, as in the cities of Eastern and Western Europe, it was mentioned that a certain Romanian "official" was good because he was "taking," that is, he allowed himself to be bought in order to be more understanding toward the Jewish minority and its specific concerns. But I ignored the fact that these were not anecdotes and isolated incidents but a true system, a well-conceived and calculated policy: the country became richer by allowing its Jews to leave. Through its government security services, the Romanian treasury received a certain amount of money—coldly calculated according to a precise schedule—for each of its Jewish citizens who wished to emigrate. Everything took place in great secrecy, far from the eyes of the media, especially under the rule of dictator Nicolae Ceausescu, who supervised the bargaining personally but at a distance. Special envoys came from Europe carrying hundreds of thousands of dollars for the Romanians.

Where was the money coming from? From American Jewish sources. Who were the liaisons of the Israeli government? Israeli agents, considered heroes in Jerusalem. But the Romanians also dealt with a British Jewish merchant who had his friends in official circles in Bucharest. Less idealistic than the Israelis, he requested a commission for his services: a troubling and at the same time fascinating episode. One reads it like a mystery. (In a quasi-comic incident, a high-ranking officer of the Romanian espionage services disguised as a Romanian "diplomat" carried a suitcase from Zurich to Bucharest; it and its contents of one million dollars were lost—and luckily found one week later.)

With honesty and evident pain, you raise profound ethical questions: in a desperate situation one could pay the Gestapo in Bratislava and Budapest extraordinary amounts of money in order to have them stop sending Slovak and Hungarian Jews to Auschwitz; but was money needed to negotiate with the Communist devil or his representatives, or in fact with a Jew who was concerned more with money than with his brothers and sisters in prison? After discussion at the highest level in Israel, Ben-Gurion ultimately decided that in order to save lives, one could deal with a scoundrel.

You had access to the witnesses and the actors in this drama and to the official archives in preparing this work: you used them with the same talent and lucidity that may also be found in your earlier book, *The Holocaust in Romania*, in which you related the sufferings of your fellow countrymen during the darkness of the Holocaust.

Nevertheless you and I must acknowledge the recent changes that have occurred in this country where political and intellectual leaders have decided finally to confront this chapter of their past: Romania is no longer the country of yesterday, even less the country of before yesterday.

Of course Ion Antonescu is still too popular in certain circles; his fanatical heritage has not completely disappeared. But in the higher levels of the government, one can see a desire to part with his legacy and conceive a nobler future, without erasing the somber traces left in history by our common enemies.

ELIE WIESEL

I am God, your God who took you

out of Egypt and out of slavery.

THE FIRST OF THE TEN COMMANDMENTS

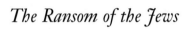

The Ransom of the Jews

Introduction:
Lost and Found

In 1974 a Romanian passenger carrying a diplomatic passport boarded a plane at the Zurich airport bound for Bucharest. The flight went smoothly, but once in Bucharest the diplomat realized with horror that one of his suitcases—one that had been given to him by an old acquaintance shortly before his departure—was missing. The Romanian diplomat was General Gheorghe Marcu, one of the division heads of the Directorate of Foreign Intelligence (DGIE), the espionage branch of the feared Securitate, the Romanian Communist regime's secret police.

The old acquaintance who had handed Marcu the suitcase was Shaike Dan, a senior adviser to several prime ministers of Israel and one of the most respected operatives of the Israeli intelligence community. The missing suitcase contained $1 million in cash, money given to Marcu in exchange for allowing a certain number of Romanian Jews to emigrate to Israel. To General Marcu's great fortune, the suitcase was found intact a few days later in the Zurich airport.[1]

For many years General Marcu was the third-ranking agent in Romanian foreign intelligence.[2] Stationed in London under diplomatic cover in the late fifties and early sixties, he also had extensive Middle East experience. The fact that his colleagues accused Marcu on more than one occasion of being a British or an Israeli spy did not seem to hinder his career.[3] In 1975, a year after losing the suitcase containing the cash, he was made head of the DGIE currency department.[4] In 1978 the forty-two-year-old Marcu supervised the DGIE division responsible for coordinating the entire Romanian espionage effort in the United States, Latin America, Asia, Africa, and the Middle East.[5] Officially he was deputy director of the Institute for World Economy. In fact, according to Cornel Burtica, minister of foreign trade and a member of the Politburo of the Romanian Communist party (RCP), this institute employed "a few dozen genuine researchers and a few hundred undercover Securitate officers."[6]

Born in 1910 in Lipcani, Bessarabia, Shaike Dan was one of the most efficient operatives in charge of *alyah beth*, the organized emigration of the Jews to Palestine and, after 1948, to Israel. In a letter addressed to Dan on the occasion of his retirement, Shimon Peres, then prime minister of Israel, wrote: "I am one of the very few people who know the truth that you did everything to hide: that without you, without your mighty devotion and your unmatched ingenuity and resourcefulness, the State of Israel would never have arrived at what it is today. Even if we distribute the credit in the fairest way possible—without your mighty undertaking that continued uninterrupted for forty years—the Jews of Romania, Yugoslavia, Bulgaria, and the Soviet Union,

600,000 olim, the cream of the Jewish people, would never have reached Israel."[7]

The 1974 Zurich meeting between Shaike Dan and General Marcu had been preceded by many other meetings and was followed by still others. The episode of the missing cash-filled suitcase was only a comic footnote in the tale of one of the greatest barters of human beings in the twentieth century: the selling of Romanian Jews to Israel.

I

"The Jews Are Our Misfortune": Anti-Semitism in Romania, from the Congress of Berlin to World War II

The history of Romanian anti-Semitism is long and sad, and to this day largely unrecognized even by most Romanians.

Following the war fought by Romania and tsarist Russia against Turkey in 1877, and after the Congress of Berlin in 1878, the nations of Europe recognized the independence of Romania. But the Congress required that Romania treat all its citizens, including Jews, as equals under the law. Article 44 of the treaty stipulated that a person's religion could not be used as a basis for denying him either his civil and political rights or his access to specific professions.

But the Congress of Berlin had little effect on the Romanian government's continuing history of discrimination against its Jewish population. Romania agreed to Article 44, but not for long. It soon required the "naturalization" of

Jews on an individual basis before the full rights of citizenship might be granted. On January 17, 1879, the Romanian
Parliament revised the country's 1866 constitution to re-
quire both an individual petition and a parliamentary vote
in order to gain naturalization, a requirement that remained
law until 1919. Thus between 1866 and 1904 only 2,000
Jews were naturalized in all of Romania. (Jewish veterans of
the 1877 War of Independence received citizenship, but
they numbered a mere 888.)[1] Romanian Jews remained
stateless and highly susceptible to both economic and political discrimination.

From the Congress of Berlin well into the twentieth
century, a large portion of the Romanian political and intellectual classes continued to express their hostility toward the
Jews and toward Article 44, the treaty provision that was intended to protect them. Resentment of the Jews in the late
nineteenth century came both from the boyars (the gentry)
and the new bourgeoisie who had recently begun to assume
a political role. As long as Jews worked as middlemen—
tax collectors, distributors of manufactured goods, and
salesmen for spirits whose production was controlled by the
boyars—they were allowed some rights. But as soon as they
showed a desire to take up other pursuits and to gain civil
and political rights, they became a "social peril," the "plague
of the countryside."

Jews had long been active in a wide range of trades in
Romania. Competition from skilled Jewish craftsmen stim-
ulated the new Christian bourgeoisie to brutal opposition of
Jewish citizenship and the support of measures that would
restrict them to "national labor." Rural peasants, living in
abject misery because of a severe land shortage, also found
the Jews easy targets for their grievances. Unable to resolve

their severe agrarian problems, and willing to pander to the nationalist feelings of Christian tradesmen and merchants, in the last decades of the nineteenth century Romanian governments were content to divert feelings of frustration and anger onto the Jews.

Carol Iancu has summarized the legal situation of the Jews at the outbreak of the 1877 War of Independence, before the Congress of Berlin: "They did not have the right to reside permanently in the countryside, and they could be expelled [from the countryside and even cities] on charges of vagrancy following an administrative order. They could own neither house, nor land, nor vineyards, nor hotels, nor taverns in the countryside; they could not possess land for cultivation; they could not sell tobacco; their right to own houses or buildings in the cities was always challenged; they could not take part in any public adjudication; they could not become professors, lawyers, pharmacists, state-certified doctors, or railroad employees; they were obliged to serve in the military, but were barred from becoming officers."[2]

Discrimination had eventually barred Jews from jobs in the railroads, the customs service, the state-run salt and tobacco monopolies, and the stock market. The 1866 constitution had permitted only Romanians (including naturalized subjects) to purchase real estate in rural areas while an 1869 law had forbidden Jews to collect taxes there. In 1884 itinerant merchants were barred from the villages, a measure that adversely affected many Jews. Several regulations hindered Jews from obtaining licenses to sell alcoholic beverages in rural settings.

The most dramatic form of anti-Semitism in rural areas was the expulsion of thousands of Jewish families from the countryside during the last third of the century by both central and local authorities. Even if they were elderly or born in the locality, those expelled were permitted only a day to leave, as when twenty-five Jewish families were forced from their homes in the Bacau district in 1885. If a Jew dared to protest Romanian anti-Semitism, he was deported.

In June 1868 military service had become compulsory for all males in Romania with the exception of foreigners. Since resident Jews were generally classed as "foreigners," this directive meant that the army would lose a source of cannon fodder and manpower. A March 1876 law on recruitment therefore stipulated that all male *residents* were obligated to serve—in other words, that only *citizens* of other nations might avoid service. Jews had thus become subject to the draft even though they were not citizens but were merely "stateless foreigners" or "inhabitants of the country." This 1876 law continued to be enforced even after the Congress of Berlin and the recognition of Romania by the European powers.

Two pieces of legislation in 1893, the Primary Education Law and the Secondary and Higher Education Law, made education free for the "sons of Romanians" only. "Foreigners" such as Jews might enroll, but only if space were available and they paid tuition.

In the late nineteenth century and the early twentieth, this continuing anti-Semitism combined with poverty to create the conditions for the mass emigration of Jews from Romania. Between 1899 and 1914, 140,000 Romanian Jews left the country.[3] Many of them traveled by foot and begged for money and food from the Jewish communities they found along their way.

Concerned about its image abroad and the risks this posed to its ability to secure foreign loans, in 1900 the

Romanian government attempted to show that its treatment of Romanian Jews was not at all harsh and that the massive emigration was the work of Jewish "provocateurs."[4] Meanwhile, especially in Bucharest, emigrating Jews were rounded up en masse in order to declare in writing that they were leaving the country because of hunger and poverty, not persecution.

A fateful transformation in Romanian politics occurred at the close of World War I, when the demographic composition of Greater Romania changed dramatically. It acquired (actually reacquired) Bessarabia from Russia as well as Transylvania and Bukovina from the Austro-Hungarian Empire. From an almost ethnically homogeneous nation-state, Romania suddenly became a country in which ethnic minorities comprised almost 30 percent of the population. In December 1918, under Western pressure, Romania abolished the humiliating requirement of parliamentary confirmation for Jewish citizenship; henceforth proof of birth in the country and evidence that the individual was not a citizen of another would suffice.

While the Romanian political classes were pleased to acquire these new territories, they were less sanguine about the minorities who inhabited them. Political leaders—especially those in the Liberal party—sought to postpone the granting of civil rights to all minorities in the new territory of Greater Romania. Again, under strong Western pressure that threatened to withhold recognition of the new Romanian borders, a new constitution was adopted. Enacted in March 1923, it granted full citizenship to Jews and other minorities. Article 56 of the Citizenship Law of 1924 extended Romanian citizenship to all inhabitants of Bessarabia, Bukovina, Transylvania, and other areas.

In a sense, the ensuing period between 1923 and 1937 represented a golden age of human rights for Romanian Jews. But unease began to appear in the mid-1930s with the formation of such nationalistic movements as the League for National Christian Defense (LANC) and the Iron Guard. Anti-Semitism was a main feature of their programs: LANC used the swastika as a political symbol, and both LANC and the Iron Guard were involved in the devastation of synagogues, the burning of Jewish homes, and the beatings of Jews.

In December 1937 the radical anti-Semitic right took power in Romania. The National Christian Party (PNC), successor to LANC, was asked by King Carol II to form a new government, even though the party had won only 9 percent of the popular vote in that year's elections. Almost immediately the civil liberties for which Jews had struggled for generations were seriously undermined by anti-Semitic legislation. As many as 200,000 Jews were immediately deprived of their civil rights. The PNC government, better known as the Goga-Cuza regime, had a short life of only forty-two days and was followed by the royal dictatorship of Carol II. But the PNC's legislative legacy endured. In August 1940, Prime Minister Ion Gigurtu, Minister of Justice Ion V. Gruia, and King Carol II signed law number 2650, openly inspired by the Nuremberg racial laws. The law defined who was to be considered a Jew; a corollary law forbade marriages between Jews and Romanians "by blood." These and other anti-Semitic measures formed legal precedents that would soon be useful to the fascist regimes that followed.

On September 6, 1940, Ion Antonescu, in an alliance with the Iron Guard, established a dictatorship which abolished the rights of the Jews still further. The war and the Nazi model of anti-Semitic public policy gave Antonescu the opportunity to radically "resolve" the "Jewish question" in Romania. From mid-1940 to early 1942 the Romanian government issued a broad range of laws and regulations with clear anti-Semitic intent.

Eighteen days after taking power, in an interview with the Italian newspaper *La Stampa*, Antonescu laid out the underlying concepts that would guide Romania's anti-Jewish economic legislation. Jews formed the greatest obstacle to expansion of the Romanian economy, Antonescu declared, and he promised to solve the problem by replacing Jews with Romanians. He proposed that most Jewish property be expropriated in exchange for compensation.

In late 1940 and early 1941 the government enacted restrictions on Jewish business activities. It prohibited Jews from engaging in the sale of products included in state monopolies—salt, matches, and tobacco, for example—while the Ministry of Labor required Jewish-owned grocery stores to remain closed on Sundays so they might not take business away from Romanian shops on the other six days of the week.[5]

Jews were eliminated from most of the professions. In November 1940, Jewish doctors and other health-care providers were excluded from the National Association of Physicians. Jewish physicians were segregated in their own professional associations and permitted to care only for Jewish patients. Dozens of professional and social associations expelled Jewish members: bar associations, the journalists' union, the writers' union, the Society of Architects, the Romanian opera, even the deaf-mute association. Segregated Jewish schools were established. An October 1940 decree provided that Jews could no longer be teachers or students.

Professional and enforced social discrimination went hand in hand with ministerial orders that essentially outlawed the recognition of Jews as human beings. By mid-1941, for example, Jews were permitted to buy bread but forbidden to purchase pastries. Beginning in August 1942, Jews were charged a higher price for bread than non-Jews, and they might purchase bread only with specially marked ration cards.[6]

While expropriations of property could be carried out with some degree of efficiency, replacing Jews in the workforce was more difficult. Although officially most Jews were fired from their jobs in 1943, thousands continued to work for Romanian firms. These companies were forced to seek every possible sort of waiver and approval in order to retain their Jewish workers, because the Jews' skills were irreplaceable; even a "Romanized" economy could not do without their services.[7]

Another key component of the fascists' anti-Semitic legislation was Jewish forced labor. As early as December 1940 the government decreed that Jews were obligated to work "in the public interest" under the Ministry of National Defense or other state ministries.

The Holocaust in Romania brought not only plunder, "Romanization," and forced labor to Romanian Jews; it culminated in a series of devastatingly cruel deportations, executed under murderous conditions. Ion Antonescu was chiefly responsible for designating the Jews as Romania's primary enemy and in ordering these deportations. His obsession with the need to purge the country of Jews was constant. On July 4, 1941, he asserted that "the Jewish people had embezzled and impoverished, speculated on and impeded the development of the Romanian people for several centuries; the need to free us from this plague is self-evident."[8] On September 6, in a letter to his deputy, Mihai Antonescu, he advised that "everyone should understand that this is not a struggle with the Slavs but with the Jews. It is a fight to the death. Either we will win and the world will purify itself, or they will win and we will become their slaves. . . . The war in general and the fight for Odessa especially have proven that Satan is the Jew."[9] On November 14, in a meeting of the Council of Ministers, Ion Antonescu declared: "I have enough difficulties with those jidani [kikes] that I sent to the Bug. Only I know how many died on their way."[10] Observing that even Nazi Germany was acting slowly, Antonescu urged his lieutenants to hasten Romania's solution to its "Jewish question": "Put them in the catacombs, put them in the Black Sea. I don't want to hear anything. It does not matter if 100 or 1,000 die, [for all I care] they can all die."[11]

Administrative and legal measures authorized the deportations, expulsions, and resettlements in ghettos. As a consequence, the entire Jewish population of Bessarabia and almost all of that of northern Bukovina were deported or "evacuated"; so was the entire rural Jewish population of Moldova. "Evacuations" were carried out primarily in northern Moldavia and southern Transylvania but also in Walachia. Transit camps and ghettos were established in Bessarabia, Bukovina, and Transnistria.

In 1930 Romania had been home to 759,000 Jews. At the close of World War II about 375,000 of them had survived. As a result of 1944 deportations to concentration camps and extermination centers in the Greater Reich,

150,000 of the original Jewish population of Romania ended up under Hungarian sovereignty in northern Transylvania. Nearly all of these—130,000—perished before the war's end. More than 45,000 Jews—probably closer to 60,000—were killed in 1941 in Bessarabia and Bukovina by Romanian and German troops. At least 75,000 of the deported Romanian Jews died as a result of expulsions to Transnistria. In all, at least 270,000 Jews under Romanian jurisdiction died, either on the explicit orders of Romanian officials or as a consequence of their criminal barbarity. Romanian officials sometimes worked with German help, but more often they acted on their own.

The general policy toward Jews during the war was one of terror, plunder, rape, deportation, and murder. Those Jews who survived owed their good fortune only to the inefficient and corrupt nature of the Romanian administrative system, to Ion Antonescu's decision to postpone and then abandon plans to deport Jews from Old Romania, and sometimes to the kindness and courage of a few Romanians.

The idea of the forced emigration of Jews was not new to Europe; it had found widespread support among both fascist and non-fascist anti-Semites in many European countries during the period between the world wars. Even the Nazis had seriously promoted such a solution before 1939. In principle the Antonescu regimes permitted the voluntary emigration of the Jews. Even the viciously anti-Semitic Iron Guards supported it. But as Antonescu instituted his wartime policies of the physical destruction of the Jews, his government was already considering how it might use their suffering to extort money from American Jewish organizations.

Romanian authorities were not content to rob the Jews of their property; they sought to extract as much value as they could from the Jews through taxes and bribery. Their devices were well known abroad. According to the Israeli historian Tuvia Friling, in late 1942 Romanian authorities asked 200,000 to 500,000 *lei* for each of the 70,000 Jews to be released from Transnistria and allowed to emigrate to Palestine. Rumors of total ransoms varied from $14 million to $48 million. David Ben-Gurion was suspicious of Romania's real intentions but willing to try to save the deportees; in British government circles the talk was of "blackmail, extortion, and slave trading."[12] When news of the would-be trade was leaked to the press, the Committee for a Jewish Army of Stateless and Palestinian Jews (CJA), a Zionist organization in New York, placed an ad in the *New York Times* of February 16, 1943, which stated bluntly: "For Sale to Humanity, 70,000 Jews, Guaranteed Human Beings at $50 Apiece." The ad continued: "Romania is tired of killing Jews. It has killed 100,000 in two years. Romania will give Jews away practically for nothing. Seventy thousand Jews are waiting in Romanian concentration camps: Romania will give these 70,000 Jews to the Four Freedoms for 20,000 Lei ($50) apiece. This sum covers all transportation expenses. . . . Attention America, the Great Romanian Bargain is for this month only."[13]

Just three days earlier, C. L. Sulzberger had written in the *Times*, quoting neutral sources in London, that the Romanian government was allegedly ready to release seventy thousand Jews from Transnistria and to permit them to depart for Palestine against "a tax of 20,000 lei on each refugee."[14] Both Sulzberger's report and the ad clearly referred to the seventy thousand Jews from Bessarabia and

Bukovina who were dying in the camps and ghettos of Transnistria, to which they had been deported by Ion Antonescu during the fall of 1941. According to Romanian official figures, not many more than fifty thousand of these Jews were alive in September 1943.

Part of the reason for the *Times* ad was the hope that publicity would help accelerate emigration to Palestine— not a simple matter. In 1943 Romanians were caught between their ardent desire to rid the country of Jews (if possible at the greatest financial and political profit) and the pressure of their German ally to exterminate them. Combined with British reluctance to allow such large numbers of Jews to settle in Palestine, the Transnistria rescue plan fell through.[15]

As the Romanian Jewish writer Mihail Sebastian wrote as early as 1941, Romanian authorities knew that the U.S. government was keeping a close eye on the mass murder and mistreatment of Romanian Jews: "Gunther, the American envoy . . ., told someone yesterday that at the peace conference the Romanians would not be forgiven two things: that they crossed the Dniester, and that they behaved as they did toward the Jews."[16] Indeed, Franklin Gunther Mott, chief of the American consulate in Bucharest, had written in August 1940 to Secretary of State Cordell Hull: "I have even availed myself of every suitable occasion to General Antonescu and other Romanian officials how deeply my Government and the people of United States deplore and abhor the exercise of wanton license in dealing with human lives. . . ."[17] Later in the war, allowing Jewish emigration would be one more way by which Romanian authorities attempted to gain favor with Washington.

In early 1944 the U.S. government made a major shift in its policy toward the fate of European Jewry. As Ira Hirschmann, a member of the newly established War Refugee Board, wrote, President Roosevelt had instructed U.S. representatives abroad "to take all measures within the Government's power to rescue the victims of the enemy persecution who are in imminent danger of death."[18] Roosevelt's choice to direct the War Refugee Board was John W. Pehle. In his office at the Treasury Department, Pehle discussed the refugee situation with Hirschmann, a former senior executive with Saks Fifth Avenue and Bloomingdale's in New York, now FDR's special representative in Turkey. Hirschmann's mission was to try to save as many Romanian, Hungarian, and Bulgarian Jews as possible. The first designated target was Transnistria.

"John Pehle was pointing at a large wall map," Hirschmann recalled. "His finger was on an area between the Bug and the Dniester rivers. . . . 'One hundred and seventy-five thousand Jews and other anti-fascists from major cities have been sent here by the Romanians,' he continued. 'It's disease infested, and only fifty thousand remain alive. See what you can do about it.'"[19]

Hirschmann saw no other option than to attempt to negotiate with the enemy for the release of the Jews at a time when Allied planes were bombing Romanian oil fields and cities.[20] By special sanction from Washington, he was permitted to do so.[21] He arranged a meeting with Alexandru Cretzianu, the Romanian minister in Ankara. Hirschmann knew that Cretzianu was sympathetic to the Allies and that his father had been a diplomat in the United States in the early 1920s.

For Cretzianu, the topic of the meeting with Hirschmann was no surprise. From remarks by the Jewish Agency representative in Turkey and by the U.S. minister Mott, Cretzianu was aware of the West's "unfavorable" reaction to the treatment of Romanian Jews.[22]

At their meeting in March 1944, Hirschmann told Cretzianu that Washington was "outraged by the reports we have received of the massacre of your own citizens. . . . There is a time when the conscience of free people will rise against barbarism and strike down the perpetrators of the crime. . . . A day of reckoning is approaching. You cannot avoid it."[23]

Cretzianu tried to defend his government by blaming the Nazis for most of the crimes (which was false) and by noting that the situation of the Romanian Jews had lately improved (which was correct). But, Hirschmann responded, "A great deal of improvement will be necessary before you will be accepted by the humane nature of the world as a self-respecting people."[24]

After further conversation, Hirschmann sensed Cretzianu's point of vulnerability. "My clue came after a casual conversation about the Russians. . . . I could see a shadow pass over his face. Suddenly he said: 'It's the Russians we fear, not the Americans.' This is what I had been looking for. Dropping all caution and with it all formality, I looked straight into Cretzianu's eyes and coldly, almost brutally, said: 'Mr. Minister, you, Antonescu, and your families are going to be killed.'

"He winced, but I continued in the same vein: 'The Russians will do it.'

"After a pause during which neither of us said a word, I resumed: 'I will offer you a visa for every member of your family in exchange for one simple act which will cost you nothing.' 'And what is that?' he queried. 'Open the door of the camp in Transnistria.' He seemed genuinely shocked. 'And why does the president of the United States send a personal representative to negotiate for some Jews?' 'That is why the United States is what it is,' I continued, 'and that is why Romania is where it is today.'"[25]

At this point it became clear to Hirschmann that the Romanian government was ready to sell its Jews. Only the price remained to be discussed. Cretzianu asked, "Precisely what do you want and what do you offer?" Hirschmann replied that the U.S. government wanted the Transnistria camp disbanded, with its Jews allowed to return to their homes immediately; that five thousand children be transported to ships that would take them to Istanbul and then to Palestine; and that Antonescu end all persecution and repression of minorities in Romania.

"It is not impossible," Cretzianu replied. "But what will you offer in return?" Hirschmann answered: "It should not be necessary to offer anything to a government to have it stop killing its citizens, but I promise you visas for entrance to the United States for you and three members of your family."[26] Soon five ships were carrying about three thousand Jewish orphans and refugees from Transnistria to Palestine.

If the Antonescu regimes allowed the emigration of the Jews, not many of them were in fact able to leave Romania. A great many of those who left perished on their way to Palestine, their vessels sunk by Soviet or German warships. Others were arrested by the British and interned on Cyprus. During the fall of 1940 the Antonescu regime allowed the departure from Romanian ports toward Palestine of three ships carrying 3,351 German Jews originating from the Reich. From September 6, 1940, to August 23, 1944, the same regime permitted seventeen ships with 4,987 Jews (mostly Romanian) to sail toward Palestine from Romanian ports; of these, 1,136 drowned with the sinking of the *Struma* (762 dead in February 1942) and the *Mefkura* (374 dead in August 1944).[27] The *Struma* was torpedoed by a Soviet submarine; only 1 person survived. The *Mefkura* was shelled by a Soviet warship; only 5 survived its sinking.

During his stay in Turkey, Hirschmann was well aware of the work of the Jewish Agency and of the Alyah Beth Mossad in Istanbul. Headed by Ben-Gurion, the Jewish Agency had intelligence ties (through Moshe Sharett, Reuven Shiloah, Teddy Kollek, and Gideon Raphael) with British military intelligence (MI9), headed by Major Tony Symonds and headquartered in Cairo.[28] Alyah Beth Mossad was a Jewish underground organization designed to support "illegal" immigration. It worked to rescue Jews from German-occupied areas and bring them to Palestine.[29] The head of Alyah Beth Mossad was Shaul Avigur, who advocated the parachuting of Alyah Beth agents into occupied Europe. Like Hirschmann, in the spring of 1944 Avigur was also stationed in Istanbul.

Hirschmann referred to the Istanbul representatives of the Alyah Beth fondly as "the boys." They had established a number of intelligence contacts in occupied Europe in order to gather information about the most efficient ways to smuggle out Jews targeted for destruction. Officially London and Washington did not cooperate with "the boys," but highly placed British and American intelligence operatives placed great value on their resourcefulness. They exchanged services and favors. Allied intelligence gained information about conditions inside enemy territory and sometimes used Palestinians as couriers to the Axis countries. The British, in turn, did not interfere with the work of Alyah Beth in making deals with shipowners and captains. Moreover, British and American intelligence officers helped "the boys" find new contacts and trained the Palestinians who were to be dropped into Axis Europe in the techniques of parachute jumping and undercover work.[30]

One of the Alyah Beth people, who parachuted into Romania in June 1944 from an RAF bomber, dressed in a British uniform, was Shaike Dan. Dan had left Romania in 1935 for Palestine. There he had joined the Nir-Am kibbutz, later returned once to Romania as a Zionist activist, and in 1941 had enlisted in an artillery unit of the British army. Dropped into Romania in 1944 together with Menu Ben-Ephraim, another Alyah Beth parachutist, Dan had two missions, one from MI9 and the other from Alyah Beth. The MI9 mission was to locate British and American pilots and crewmen who were being held as prisoners of war in Romania. The Romanian oil fields had been heavily bombed by the RAF and the U.S. Air Force, and hundreds of downed British and American crewmen had been captured and held by the Romanian army, first in Poiana Tapului and then in Bucharest. British and U.S. headquarters had no information of the whereabouts of the airmen and were eager to know about the conditions of their internment. The Alyah Beth portion of the mission was to establish contact with the Zionist leadership in Bucharest, to organize Jewish self-defense there (the danger of German and Romanian mass reprisals against the Jews was still great), and to speed the emigration of Jews to Palestine.

After parachuting into Romania with Ben-Ephraim, Dan worked his way to Bucharest where he contacted the emissaries of various underground Zionist organizations and tried to mediate among them.[31] A representative of the Zionist underground, Yitzhak Artzi, become Dan's contact and helped him and Menu Ben-Ephraim with false papers. Soon the two men located the camps where British and American prisoners were being held and procured their names. This information was transmitted immediately to MI9 in Cairo.

Dan then began his mission on behalf of Alyah Beth. He was facing German pressures against emigration, Romanian opportunism and greed, conflicts between underground Jewish leaders, and the shifting attitudes of the Turkish government. (Turkish waters were extremely important for the transit of departing ships.) Nevertheless Dan, together with the clandestine Jewish leadership from Romania, was able to arrange for three ships—the *Morina*, the *Bulbul*, and the *Mefkura*—altogether loaded with slightly more than a thousand Jewish emigrants, to leave for Palestine in August 1944, sailing from the Romanian port of Constanta. Only the *Morina* and the *Bulbul* reached their destination.

When Dan parachuted into Romania, the Romanian government was desperately looking for a way out of its alliance with Nazi Germany in order to avoid occupation by Soviet troops. Toward this end, Romanian authorities believed the Romanian Jewish leadership to be so powerful that it was capable of convincing the Allies to open a second front in the Balkans. Panic over the Soviets was so great that during the night of August 22–23, 1944, Ovidiu Vladescu, general secretary of the Romanian government, on Mihai Antonescu's behalf, asked A. L. Zissu and Wilhelm

Filderman, leaders of the clandestine Jewish leadership, to request that the U.S. and British Allies occupy Romania before the Russians.[32] This was naive, wishful thinking. Less than twenty-four hours later, King Michael, with the support of the National Peasant, Liberal, Social Democratic, and Communist parties, arrested Ion Antonescu and declared Romania on the side of the Allies.

The political situation following this coup was, as Dan described it, "fluid." The next day (Dov) Berl Schieber, an emissary of Menu Ben-Ephraim, went to see Emil Bodnaras, an NKVD agent and head of the Communist militia in charge of defending Bucharest, to suggest that the Zionist underground would cooperate with the new government.[33] Meanwhile, heavy German attacks against Bucharest were blunted by U.S. and British bombings. A week later the Red Army reached Bucharest. After further communication between Dan and British authorities in Cairo, Allied planes landed in Bucharest and transported the British and American prisoners out of Romania to safety. Dan then changed into a crisp British uniform and remained behind in Romania. A new phase of *alyah* was beginning.

2

Voting with Their Feet: Jewish Emigration Before the Fall of the Iron Curtain

With the support of the Red Army and the Soviet secret services, the Romanian Communist party began immediately to consolidate its power by taking over key ministries of government and gradually but ruthlessly eliminating from Romanian political life anyone who dared oppose its goals. For the foreseeable future, democracy in Romania was doomed.

In October 1944, in a meeting in the Kremlin, Churchill and Stalin settled the postwar spheres of influence between the Western Allies and the Soviet Union in the Balkans and Eastern Europe. The British proposal, approved by Stalin with a stroke of his blue pencil, gave the Western Allies a 90 percent influence in Greece, a 50 percent influence in Yugoslavia and Hungary, 25 percent in Bulgaria, and only 10 percent in Romania. In practical terms this meant that the influence of the Western Powers in governing Romania would be minimal, next to nothing, while the USSR would have an overwhelming dominance.[1] The National Peasant party and the Romanian Communist party, uncompromising adversaries in the immediate post–World War II struggle for political power in Romania (the first backed by the Western powers, the second by the USSR), found themselves competing for the favor of the Iron Guard's "former untainted members" who were now perceived as potentially useful militants. Anti-Semitism was therefore very much alive.

Beginning in 1945, Romanian war criminals were tried at the request not only of the Jewish victims of the Holocaust but also of the U.S., British, and Soviet governments and by prominent members of the National Peasant and Communist parties. On January 21, 1945, the so-called Law 50, pertaining to the punishment of war criminals, was drafted by the Romanian minister of justice and signed by King Michael. Four of the accused were found guilty and executed in Romania: Ion Antonescu; his deputy Mihai Antonescu; C. Z. Vasiliu, the former deputy head of the Romanian ministry of interior; and Gheorghe Alexianu, former governor of Transnistria. But in dozens of cases, the death sentences of civil servants and high-ranking officers were commuted by the courts or other legal bodies. On June 1, for example, the minister of justice asked the king to commute capital punishment for twenty-nine of the accused in the first trial of war criminals, and the king agreed.[2] Hundreds of officers and high-ranking officials were sentenced to life or lengthy prison terms. Hundreds of noncommissioned officers, gendarmes, and enlisted men were also sentenced to prison terms or hard labor. Those who did not die in prison were released between 1958 and 1962. The publicity surrounding the first trials was used by the Romanian

Communist party as propaganda against its political enemies; but as the party tightened its grip on power, this propaganda faded and eventually vanished altogether.

The close of World War II represented a miracle of sorts
for the Jewish population of Romania: at least 350,000 Jews,
most of them from Regat (Romania in its pre–World War I
borders), survived the Holocaust. With the exception of the
Soviet Union, Romania now had the greatest number of
Jews in all of Europe.

In order to avoid direct Soviet rule, Holocaust survivors
from Bessarabia and Bukovina were frantically attempting
to make their way to Regat, even though the Jews there
found themselves severely impoverished. The new governments were incapable or unwilling to initiate the restitution
of properties that had been confiscated by the Antonescu
regime. Although sympathetic to the survivors of the Holocaust, Lucretiu Patrascanu, the Communist minister of justice, declared that he could not help them recover their
property because he feared the reaction of those massive
numbers who had profited from Aryanization. Iuliu Maniu,
the democratic leader of the National Peasant party who
was "committed to the idea that moral limits should restrain
ethnic resentments," told a group of Jewish leaders in 1946:
"For now the state has more important problems than the
Jewish question. . . . And anyway, how serious are your
problems? You have been able to manage [so far] with your
money and your brains."[3]

Meanwhile Romanian Jews were hearing further warn-
ings from fellow Jews and from Red Army soldiers, advis-
ing them to move as quickly and as far as possible from

"big brother." The mass emigration to Palestine was just over the horizon.

As the late chief rabbi of Romania, Moses Rosen, recalled in his memoirs, for many of the survivors "the only way to make a new start in life was to take the road to the Land of Israel. They no longer trusted anyone—and with reason. If they were to go on living, they had to become masters of their own fate and that of their children, to live normal and independent lives. Ships were sailing for Palestine crammed with these desperate Jews. The Jewish masses eagerly awaited these ships and Jewish youth craved for the unique opportunity of being reborn to a life worth living: *alyah* to the Land of Israel."[4]

Adding to the pressures, the Red Army began rounding up Jewish refugees from Bessarabia and Bukovina, considered by the USSR to be Soviet citizens, in order to move them back to the regions from which they had fled. According to Liviu Rotman, "Ironically, the Soviet authorities conferred prisoner-of-war status on many Jews they found on the front lines who had been in forced labor in Transnistria and other deportation regions. Many 'prisoners' were not released despite appeals by their families and various Jewish communities against this outrageous situation, stressing their serious physical and moral condition."[5] Immediately after the successful coup against Antonescu, looking for information on the whereabouts of his family from Lipcani, Shaike Dan visited an orphanage in Bucharest where he witnessed "the orphans of Transnistria . . . blank-faced . . . children whose eyes screeched with the horrors of the Holocaust. . . . I knew I had to smuggle out these Transnistria orphans before they fell into the hands of the Red Army, which was getting closer, otherwise they would

be sent back to Transnistria."[6] Taken back to the USSR in
1945 by Soviet authorities, one hundred of these children
were sent to orphanages in Odessa, only to be rescued once
more the next year by Rabbi Zissu Portugal of Agudath Israel, an ultra-orthodox Jewish organization. The children
were successfully returned to Romania and then sent to
Palestine and Israel.[7] Like Dan's sister Shifra, many Jews
from Bessarabia and Bukovina were able to cross clandestinely into Romania. When the border was sealed, other
Jews from the same regions made the trip via Poland. Dan's
brother Nissan escaped in this manner from Bessarabia.

Just as Jews had been blamed for modernization and for the
birth of capitalism in Romania in the nineteenth century,
now the coming of communism was laid at their feet. Without question Jews were overrepresented among the rank and
file and in the leadership structure of the Romanian Communist party, a tiny prewar organization now rapidly inflated
by a massive infusion of new members (some of them true
believers, most of them opportunists). But, as Andrei Roth
notes, "Hand in hand with the overall increase in the total
number of the party members, the proportion of the Jews
had decreased."[8] Nonetheless a daily U.S. intelligence report noted in April 1945: "Anti-Semitism is reliably reported
to be increasing among all political groups in Moldova, including the Communists."[9] Dan describes this trend in the
story of a man participating in a huge pro-Communist rally
who carried the portrait of Ana Pauker, a leading Jewish
Communist. After having his heel repeatedly stepped on by
the man next to him, he shouted, "Stop stepping on my foot,
or I'll smash your head with the *jidanca* [kike]."[10]

Under these circumstances it was only natural for Alyah Beth Mossad to concentrate on the emigration of Romanian Jews, trying to move as many as possible to Palestine. The task was extremely difficult: the British quota for Jewish emigration to Palestine was only 3,600 per year. One of the priorities of Alyah Beth Mossad was to win the goodwill of Romanian Communists toward the Jewish emigration.

The attitude of the Romanian Communist party toward Jewish emigration was ambivalent and fluctuated with Soviet policy shifts. "From 1945 to 1946," Liviu Rotman writes, "Communist representatives joined the other Jewish fractions supporting the emigration struggle, but only reluctantly acknowledged the possibility of a viable Jewish State. . . . In October and November 1945 the Communists supported the Zionist press against anti-Jewish acts in Tripolitania and Egypt and the pro-Arab stand of British Foreign Minister A. Bevin, but at the same time they refrained from firm support for a Jewish state in Palestine. With respect to *alyah* the Communists advocated free emigration to all countries, without singling out Palestine. Their position became more flexible for a short period in 1947 when they welcomed the imminent proclamation of the State of Israel. This shift in attitude was promoted by the position of the USSR, which viewed Israel as a potential center of ideological and political expansion in the Middle East."[11]

Indeed, as early as 1946 the Soviet government advocated free emigration to Palestine. In September 1946, Soviet embassies in Poland, Romania, Czechoslovakia, Bulgaria, and Hungary were instructed "not to interfere with nor to hinder the passage of Jewish refugees on their way to Palestine."[12] In order to extend their control over Romania's Jewish population, in June 1945 the Communists

there established, with the help of Iosif Sraier, an influential
fellow traveler, the Comitetul Democratic Evreiesc (CDE).
The politics of the CDE mirrored faithfully those of the
Romanian Communist party on the Jewish problem.[13]

In December 1944, as British commanders were recall-
ing Shaike Dan to Cairo,[14] Moshe Agami arrived in
Bucharest in the company of Joseph Klarmann. Agami was
a highly placed agent of the Alyah Beth Mossad; he came to
Romania with prewar experience there and an arranged position as the Romanian correspondent for the labor daily
Davar, published in Palestine. In his youth in Poland, Klarmann had actually been a journalist; now he had no difficulty in establishing himself as the Jewish Telegraphic
Agency correspondent in Bucharest.[15] Dan remembers
Agami, who "carried a valid Palestinian passport," being
driven around Bucharest in a car with a "small British flag
on it" and living in "a spacious, legal apartment [with] a
wonderful Romanian cook, and bottles of vodka for the wee
hours of the night. . . . Moshe Agami's apartment doubled
as an office for the emissaries, and as a place to get a whiff
of the spirit of the Land of Israel."[16]

In addition to the goodwill of the newly established Romanian authorities, Alyah Beth Mossad needed ships in order to effect the emigration of Jews to Palestine. Klarmann
and Agami cultivated J. D. Pandelis, the Greek owner of the
Struma, the *Smyrna*, the *Aegia Anastasia*, and other ships, as
well as the leadership of the Romanian secret services. According to Shlomo Leibovici-Lais, a member of the Zionist
underground in Romania in 1943–1948 and later an official
in the Israeli Ministry of Foreign Affairs, Klarmann introduced Agami to Emil Bodnaras, head of the Romanian secret
services.[17] Already the general secretary to the president of

the Council of Ministers, since April 1945 Bodnaras had been in charge of the feared Romanian intelligence agency, Serviciul Special de Informatii (SSI).[18] Born in 1904 of a Ukrainian father and a German mother in Bukovina, in the thirties Bodnaras had been an officer in the Romanian army who had deserted in order to became a Soviet spy.[19] Dan describes Bodnaras as "an old Communist who escaped to Russia during the old regime . . . who had a Jewish wife." Both Klarmann and Agami became friendly with Bodnaras, who was "very sympathetic" toward the Palestinian envoys, an attitude confirmed by Leibovici-Lais.[20]

After his discharge from the British army in Cairo, Dan was sent by Alyah Beth Mossad clandestinely back to Romania. After a complicated journey via Italy, Austria, and Hungary with his fellow parachutist Menu Ben-Ephraim, sometime in the early spring of 1946 he reached Bucharest and reconnected with Agami. Under Agami's leadership, and with other Alyah Beth Mossad agents, Dan continued to organize the emigration of Romanian Jews. A decision was made to send another boatload of immigrants to Palestine aboard the *Smyrna*. The operation was a complicated one. In Romania, Dan and his colleagues struggled to obtain exit permits for the Jewish immigrants over the opposition of British authorities who raised continuing obstacles. The financial demands of the shipowners and their crews, the corruption of the Romanian authorities, and the unpredictable policy shifts of the Soviet occupation authorities added to the difficulty of the task. In Paris, meanwhile, Ehud Avriel of the Alyah Beth Mossad office there was procuring thousands of Ethiopian visas from Bucharest (the lie was transparent, but the Romanian authorities did not care). Finally, after the name of the ship was changed from the *Smyrna* to the *Max Nordau* (after a World War I Zionist), 1,754 passengers sailed on May 7, 1946, from Constanta to Palestine.

Following the sailing of the *Max Nordau*, British pressures proved insurmountable, ending the illegal Jewish emigration via sea from Romania. But the Romanians continued to allow Jews to travel to Yugoslavia, where the sailings continued.[21] Alyah Beth Mossad emissaries were already on the ground in Yugoslavia working toward this goal. Together with Agami and Baruch Kamin, Dan made sure that the transit to Yugoslavia via Timisoara and Jimbolia ran smoothly: "Our friend Bodnaras . . . sent a special commissar to work with our people in the field and to prevent unforeseen problems. I myself ran back and forth between Bucharest and the Romanian-Yugoslav border, prodding Jews to assemble in Yugoslavia and get ready for *alyah* on a boat called *Hagana*."[22] With Bodnaras's blessing, and through Melania Iancu (a Zionist activist and a CDE member), Agami and Dan contacted the Romanian minister of the interior, Teohari Georgescu, and his chief officers for assurance that emigrating Jews could leave Romania without difficulty. A man named Leha, the commissar assigned to the operation, was regularly provided with "small amounts of money" and other gifts from Alyah Beth Mossad via the CDE.[23] On July 24, 1946, the *Hagana* sailed from Yugoslavia to Palestine with 2,678 Romanian Jews aboard.

The Paris office of Alyah Beth Mossad now became the operations center of the illegal emigration to Palestine. The organization's strategy was shifting toward the use of larger ships. It also provided funds for the transfer of Jews from Romania to Yugoslavia.[24] Ehud Avriel, who had good contacts with the Yugoslav security services, was one of the few people who understood early on the seriousness of the rift between the Yugoslavs and the Soviets.[25] Concerned about the situation in Romania, he advised Shaike Dan to go to Yugoslavia.

When Dan returned to Bucharest and found that emigration via sea from Romania had totally stopped, he went immediately to Yugoslavia to reassess the situation and further the emigration of the Romanian Jews in transit there. After the departure of the *Max Nordau*, a small Pandelis vessel called the *Aegia Anastasia* was prepared for sailing; but because of the new Romanian restrictions on emigration by sea, Alyah Beth Mossad arranged for the ship to be moved to the Yugoslav port of Bakar. Pandelis also supplied another, much larger ship, the *Knesset Israel*, which was soon loaded with some three thousand emigrants.[26] Both ships left Bakar on November 6, 1946. With a limited capacity of six hundred, the *Aegia Anastasia*, now renamed the *Hakedosha*, sank between Bakar and Split with no loss of human life.[27] Its passengers were transferred to the already over-crowded *Knesset Israel*, which successfully arrived in Haifa, only to have its passengers immediately deported to Cyprus by British authorities.

After these sailings, Dan established a direct contact with the head of the Yugoslav secret services (code named Stephen). Like other East European Communists, the Yugoslavs, who at that point did not allow the emigration of their own Jews to Palestine, saw the Zionists as their allies in the "anti-imperialist," anti-British struggle. Furthermore they respected Dan for his wartime deeds as a parachutist (Randolph Churchill, Winston Churchill's son, had also been parachuted into Yugoslavia during the war by the RAF to support Tito's partisans). Dan discovered that the Yugoslavs knew in detail about his *alyah* activities, and that they not only tolerated but encouraged them. In the spring of 1947 Dan established a similar relationship with the leadership of the Bulgarian secret services.

Meanwhile in Bucharest, Moshe Agami and Josef Klarmann continued to cultivate their connection with Bodnaras, who had now been elevated to minister of defense and who continued to be one of the most trusted high-ranking Soviet agents in Romania. Sometime in the fall of 1947, according to Dan, Agami and Klarmann "spoke to him about the possibility of fifteen thousand Jews emigrating at once from a port in Romania. Until then no one had talked about numbers like this, but I believed we'd be able to squeeze them onto two ships.[28]

"Bodnaras didn't turn the idea down flat. He asked for a day or two to talk it over with his superiors. Despite his senior status, he had to consult with Moscow and with its representative in Romania, Ambassador Kaftaradze. Two days later he came back with a positive reply: the ships could put in at a Romanian port, and fifteen thousand Jews would be permitted to sail aboard them. But this positive response had two qualifications: all the work on the ships to ready them for sailing would be done in Romania—and, needless to say, paid in full; and the sailing itself would take place not from Romania but from a neighboring country. . . .

"The Romanians had good reason to permit such a large number of Jews to leave. First of all, they'd be rid of some Jews, and if it looked like a shipload of fighters to help in the struggle against British imperialism, what could be better? Another reason was much more practical. Most of the Jews were not from rural areas in Romania but from big cities. The apartments they would leave behind were as important to the Romanians as air to breathe. Finally, the preparation and stocking of the ships in Romania, the astronomical sums we'd spend on building materials, fuel, water, and food, and the employment of several hundred workers in Constanta for several months, would improve Romania's foreign currency reserves by no mere trifling sum."[29]

According to Leibovici-Lais, when Bodnaras returned with a positive answer from Kaftaradze, he also added, "You asked me to let fifteen thousand people go. I advise you to take out fifty thousand. These will be the last to leave."[30] Bodnaras must have known that the Iron Curtain, anticipated by Churchill only four days after the surrender of the Third Reich, was about to fall.

But the circumstances under which the emigration of the Romanian Jews to Palestine was allowed to continue grew more complicated. Due to British pressure, the Romanians were willing to continue to allow the emigration but not through their ports, even though Alyah Beth Mossad was allowed to repair its ships there. At the same time Bulgaria was ready to open its ports to the Romanian emigrants for a fee per head. With the coordination of Shaul Avigur in Paris, Alyah Beth Mossad adapted quickly to the new situation that required larger ships, greater funding, and faster response. In this effort Dan shuttled between various East European capitals; in Bucharest, Agami busily arranged for exit permits and the bribing of various Romanian officials; in Geneva, Pinchas "Pino" Guinsburg, treasurer of Alyah Beth Mossad, paid certain fees per head to Bulgarian authorities while Ephraim Shiloh of the Tirat Zvi kibbutz coordinated transportation logistics in Bulgaria.

Meanwhile thousands of Romanian Jews were crossing the border into Bulgaria, over the Danube, through Negru

Voda and Giurgiu ports, each of them allowed to take out of the country two to three dollars per person. Again Commissar Leha, together with Commissar Chief Solomon from the Inspectoratul de Siguranta al Capitalei (ISG), supervised the departures at the two crossing points.[31] Again Moshe Agami coordinated the operation with Bunaciu of the Ministry of the Interior and Feldman of the CDE, making sure that the formal requirements imposed on the emigrants by these agencies were eased. The result of this activity was the sailing from Bulgaria on September 26, 1947, of two ships: the *Medinat Hayhudim* (formerly the U.S. icebreaker *North-land*) with 2,664 emigrants, and the *Geula* with 1,688.[32] A day earlier, two other Alyah Beth Mossad ships, the *Pan Crescent* and the *Pan York*, arrived in Constanta where work to prepare them for sea began at once.

David Ben-Gurion in Tel Aviv and Moshe Sharett in the United States now had concern that the illegal emigration to Palestine might jeopardize the creation of the state of Israel by triggering an Arab uprising and consequently a delay of the UN resolution establishing Israel. Already in Palestine and under pressure from his superiors to halt the sailing of the *Pan Crescent* and the *Pan York*, Shaul Avigur faced similar pressure from Alyah Beth Mossad to continue the sailings. He decided to approve their departure, though the preparation of the ships was heavily improvised. The ships were moved to the Bulgarian port of Burgas. After thousands of Romanian Jews crossed the Danube into Bulgaria, the *Pan York* and the *Pan Crescent*, carrying 15,239 souls, sailed on December 27, 1947, from Burgas to Palestine. As they had done with the earlier *Exodus* ship, British authorities in Cyprus interned the passengers of these two ships before they allowed them to proceed to Palestine.

During 1947 a transport of five hundred Jewish children was allowed to leave Romania legally for the Netherlands. Another two thousand Jews were allowed to leave Romania legally following individual requests. And in the same year some sixteen thousand Romanian Jews crossed the borders illegally, most of them into Hungary.[33] Three days after the sailing of the *Pan York* and the *Pan Crescent*, the Iron Curtain fell on Romania. On December 30, 1947, King Michael was forced by the Communists to abdicate.

3

The Zionist Enemy

From the close of 1947 to May 14, 1948, when David Ben-Gurion proclaimed the state of Israel, no Romanian Jews emigrated to Palestine. The United States recognized the new nation that same day, the Soviet Union two days later, and Romania on June 11. In July, Romanian authorities agreed to receive an Israeli legation in Bucharest, and, roughly four months later, agreed to receive Reuven Rubin as Israel's plenipotentiary minister. In June 1949, at a time when there were only four consulates in Israel—the United States, the Soviet Union, France, and Great Britain—Romanian diplomats arrived and opened their own.

Almost from the onset of their diplomatic relations, Israel and Romania wrangled over the subject of Jewish emigration. In March 1949, Moshe Sharett, Israel's minister of foreign affairs, wrote his counterpart, Ana Pauker—a member of the Politburo of Romania's Communist party—that the emigration of Romanian Jews to Israel, though permitted, had almost ceased. Sharett emphasized that Jewish emigration to Israel was vital to the survival of the new state.

In Romania, he protested, Zionism was presented as a "poisonous imperialist weapon" and a "reactionary and fascist force." Sharett asked that seven Palestinian emissaries, all Israeli citizens imprisoned by Romanian authorities for spreading "Zionist propaganda," be liberated, and he asked the Romanian government to reexamine its policy toward Jewish emigration to Israel.[1]

These early diplomatic relations between Romania and Israel reflected the tensions of Soviet policy. On one hand the Kremlin enlisted Israel in its "anti-imperialist front"—Moscow had thought favorably of the militant anti-British policies of the Jews in Palestine. On the other hand, Soviet Jews continued to be persecuted as part of an anti-Zionist campaign.

In 1948, as the historian Joshua Rubenstein notes, Stalin provided the essential munitions for Israel to win the war against the Arab Legion.[2] With Soviet approval, the Czech government sold massive amounts of firearms to Israel. Dan and a Russian-Romanian Jew, Robert Adam, who then lived in Paris, worked out a plan with Shaul Avigur and a future top Israeli diplomat in Prague, Ehud Avriel. The scheme allowed Israel to buy firearms from the Czech government and transport them through Yugoslavia to Israel. With the help of Avriel and Ephraim Illin, a successful Jewish businessman, who lived in Paris, Adam arranged for private American donations to Israel to be transferred to a Swiss account in his name; Adam then transferred the money to Avriel, who paid the Czechs. Although the Czech government forbade the shipping of firearms direct to Israel, it willingly allowed their transfer via Yugoslavia. Illin, Avriel, and Dan even succeeded in buying and sending military planes, including fighters, from Prague through Yugoslavia to Israel.³ Well-informed historians and political leaders in Israel today credit Illin for saving Jerusalem and perhaps Israel itself upon its creation in 1948. As described in his book *Al Hechatum* (The Undersigned), Illin arranged the sailing of the famous *SS Nora* from Venice to the port of Sibenik in Yugoslavia, and from there to Tel Aviv. The *Nora* was loaded in Yugoslavia with Czech firearms, bought by Ehud Avriel in Czechoslovakia, which proved crucial in struggles at the creation of the newly independent state. Spitfire aircraft, also bought from Czechoslovakia for the Israeli air force, were fitted with additional fuel tanks shipped via Yugoslavia to Israel—and it was Illin again who obtained the fuel for these planes. This was a delicate operation, as Stalin's relationship to Tito had grown tense around the same time.

In September 1948, Golda Meir arrived in Moscow as head of the first Israeli legation to the Soviet Union. According to Rubenstein, "Enormous crowds greeted her in front of Moscow's main synagogue on Saturday September 11, where she attended Sabbath morning services with members of her staff. . . . Several weeks later, even larger crowds assembled on Rosh Hashana and again on Yom Kippur. They waited for hours in front of the synagogue, then escorted Golda through the streets, shouting 'Next year in Jerusalem!'"⁴

Two months later the wife of foreign minister and Politburo member V. M. Molotov, Polina Zhemchuzhina, herself a Jew, encouraged Meir to continue to attend synagogue in Moscow, saying to her in Yiddish: "I am a daughter of the Jewish people."⁵ Stalin, outraged by this display of "Jewish nationalism," responded swiftly and brutally. On November 20 the Jewish Anti-Fascist Committee, created in March 1942 by the Soviet government in order to win sympathy and support from the West, was dissolved. In January 1949 the Soviet press began a vigorous "anti-cosmopolitan," anti-Jewish campaign.

Between September 1948 and January 1949 the Soviet government began arresting prominent Jewish intellectuals and activists; dissolving societies for Jewish culture in Kiev; and closing Yiddish-language journals. Polina Zhemchuzhina was arrested for her pro-Jewish sympathies. The Soviet secret police manufactured confessions to four crimes by those who had been arrested: bourgeois nationalism; creation of an anti-Soviet nationalistic underground; treason against the Soviet Union; and espionage on behalf of U.S. intelligence.[6] In May 1952 fifteen Jewish members of the Jewish Anti-Fascist Committee were thus tried, and in August thirteen were executed.

In Czechoslovakia, meanwhile, the Communist party organized, under close Soviet supervision, the viciously anti-Semitic trial of Rudolf Slansky, a former party official.

In December 1952, at a meeting of the presidium of the Politburo, Stalin declared: "Every Jew is a nationalist and an agent of American intelligence."[7] He organized a second major anti-Semitic secret police investigation and trial in January 1953 under the rubric of the "doctors' plot." A month after Stalin's death (on March 5, 1953), Soviet authorities revealed that the "doctors' plot" had been fabricated by the Soviet secret police. But Jewish doctors had been already condemned for allegedly planning to poison the Soviet leadership, and some of them had been executed.

As one of Eastern Europe's most obedient Soviet satellites, Romania closely imitated the "Soviet model" in its policies toward Romanian Jews and Israel. Because the Soviets hoped that the new state of Israel would join the "anti-imperialist camp," Soviet satellites in Eastern Europe were at first encouraged to allow Jews to emigrate to Israel. The Romanian Communist party even encouraged the emigration of Communist Jews to Israel, hoping thereby to reinforce the Israeli Communist party. Between December 1948 and January 1949, 3,600 "politically instructed" Jews left Romania for Israel in order to "support the fight against the domination of American imperialism in Israel."[8] Shlomo Leibovici-Lais recalls that one of the ships that carried these emigrants also carried typography and typesetting equipment—everything the Israeli Communist party would need to print the Romanian-language newspaper *Glasul Poporului.*[9]

Emulating the other face of the Soviet model, the Romanian Communist party began its own anti-Zionist campaign. In *The Rise and Fall of a Jewish Communist*, Robert Levy writes, "In March 1948 the [Romanian] government issued for the first time secret, never-published criteria restricting Jewish emigration from Romania . . . that formally prohibited Jews who were skilled workers . . . doctors, or engineers from emigrating."[10]

In October that year the Politburo of the Romanian Communist party twice discussed the Jewish problem. First it decided to close Jewish schools and hospitals, and in March 1949 it outlawed the American Jewish Joint Distribution Committee (popularly known as the Joint).[11] As Vasile Luca, a member of the Romanian Communist party's Politburo, recognized, the Joint had been extremely helpful in sending foodstuffs and supplies in the immediate post–World War II years, not only to Romanian Jews but to the general Romanian population, which was then confronted by severe drought and famine. Yet this made no difference to Romanian authorities, who thought of the Joint, in the words of Miron Constantinescu, another party leader, as an espionage network.

The end of the war had brought no peace to Romania's Jewish community. Desperate Jews crammed aboard "eagerly awaited" ships headed for Palestine, and, according to Moses Rosen, "Jewish youth craved the unique opportunity of being reborn to a life worth living: *alyah* to the Land of Israel." Yet Jewish Communists opposed the emigration and did their utmost to obstruct the exodus.[12]

Zionists in Romania actively promoted and helped organize the move to Palestine. As early as 1945 the Romanian Zionist Organization headquartered in Israel wrote Ana Pauker to inform her of the efforts of the Jewish leadership in Palestine to create the state of Israel.[13] Yet Jewish Communists would not budge, and they set out to destroy Romania's Union of Jews from within. First they attacked Wilhelm Filderman, an emblem of the organization, and, in a display of power, arranged for him to be briefly arrested.[14] In 1945 the Romanian Communist party established a new organization, the Jewish Democratic Committee (CDE). Although most of its founders were Communists, they included a few left-wing Zionists "to ensure the democratic unity of the Jewish population and to fight against reactionary Jewish elements, whose interests were tied to the reactionary policies of the historical parties."[15]

From the outset, the CDE sought to undermine the autonomy of Romanian Jewish institutions and to control Filderman's Union of Jews.[16] According to Moses Rosen, the Zionists offered no resistance, for they saw no future for Jews in Romania. In 1947, as Rosen and the CDE stepped up their attacks on Filderman and Chief Rabbi Safran, both men left the country.[17]

In June 1948, Rosen was elected chief rabbi of a devastated Romanian Jewish community.

Rosen had been born in 1912 in Moinesti, a small shtetl in Moldova, the son of an Orthodox rabbi of Falticeni. His brother Elias had been the rabbi of Oswiecim, later known as Auschwitz. Together with his wife and two children, Elias perished in the Holocaust. Rosen had been affiliated with the Zionists and Social Democrats before the war. Accused of being a Communist, in 1939 he was thrown into the Miercurea Ciuc camp by the regime of Carol II, along with, ironically, many members of the Iron Guard. Because of his past, Rosen was, from the Communist perspective, a natural "fellow traveler."

As chief rabbi of the Romanian Jewish community, Rosen now found himself in an odd position. On one hand he opposed the Communist party's atheistic policies, which, through the CDE, controlled and nearly destroyed the Romanian Jewish community. On the other hand he could scarcely support the Zionists, who aspired to emigrate to Israel and therefore invested little in maintaining the integrity of Romania's Jewish community.

As Rosen was profoundly concerned with the survival of the Jewish community in Romania, he had to play a dangerous political game. He sought to accommodate the Communist leadership—which wavered on the subject of Jewish emigration but advocated total assimilation—without compromising the autonomy of the Jewish community; at the same time he attempted to maintain an alliance with the Zionists without advocating a general exodus to Israel. Negotiating this political terrain sometimes made Rosen's life a nightmare. "My position at this time was rather paradoxical," he later wrote. "The Jewish Communists wanted the Jews to remain in the country, but to become totally assimilated. Therefore, even if they agreed to maintain communities, their final purpose was completely opposed to mine. On the other hand, the Zionists, my natural allies in my struggle for strong communities, saw in this struggle a danger of 'stabilization,' a danger for *alyah*. Every improvement, every concession I obtained was for them an impediment to emigration."[18]

But Rosen was not unsuccessful in achieving his aims, even during the years of the harsh Stalinist repression. On Hanukah, in December 1951, Rosen spoke to the leading Israeli diplomatic envoy in a meeting at which he was expected to criticize both the United States and the Israeli governments. Instead he directed his criticism entirely at Washington. Beginning in 1948, the Romanian secret police watched Rosen closely until communism fell in 1989.[19]

Zionist activities in Romania continued energetically. When an Israeli legation opened in Bucharest, rallies supporting Israel took place in front of the Israeli mission. The CDE tried to persuade Israeli diplomats to halt the rallies and began an anti-Zionist campaign in Romania. The Romanian Communist party, for its part, passed a resolution in November 1948 which condemned Zionism and accused Zionists of being traitors and spies.[20]

Romania's Zionists responded to these forms of persecution in two ways: they demanded the acceleration of emigration to Israel and praised the Soviet Union for helping to establish the new state. Falticeni's Zionist organization printed a poster that declared, "Jews, let us all go to the Great Synagogue today . . . to attend the rally of the Jewish population, and celebrate the historical event of the creation of the Jewish state. Nobody should miss the opportunity to show, besides the joy of the moment, our thanks and gratitude to our defenders at the UN, led by the USSR."[21]

Yet despite the large numbers of Jews that lined up each day outside the interior ministry to obtain permission to emigrate, and despite Rubin's persistent pressure on Pauker to relax emigration policies, Zionist demands came to little effect. Tensions exploded in February 1949 after a week of massive Zionist protests against Romania's emigration policies. Romanian authorities swiftly and brutally responded.

On February 18, one day after a protest by twenty thousand Jews, the regime arrested three Israeli emissaries suspected of espionage. Four other emissaries were already under arrest, detained since December 1948. Moshe Agami and other Israeli envoys avoided the CDE, which they knew carried little weight on issues related to Jewish emigration. The Zionist activist Mela Iancu recalls that "at the beginning of 1949, [Mordechai] Namir [a future Israeli diplomatic envoy to Moscow] visited Ana Pauker. Namir went with Agami, and from the [foreign] ministry came directly to me. They were very pleased. Of course we discussed the essential problem, emigration. They reported that Ana Pauker had come up with the numbers—5,000 people per month, with a total of 40,000 to 50,000 people. Namir was optimistic and hoped that this emigration would soon start. At a reception in which the minister of Israel, Rubin, participated, he asked Ana Pauker to set free the Palestinian instructors, who had already been in prison for four months." Pauker immediately entreated Teohari Georgescu, another member of the party's Politburo: "Teo, see what the story is with those Palestinian boys, and let them go." The boys were shortly set free under condition that they leave Romania immediately.[22]

On the same day the Israeli emissaries were arrested, the Romanian Communist party's secretariat directly addressed the emigration issue. Pauker and Georgescu advised their colleagues to wait for things to calm down, then begin emigrating the "elderly and those with children in Israel."[23] Vasile Luca and Gheorghe Gheorghiu-Dej, the party leader, were immovable. According to Dej, Zionist leaders "should be summoned and treated like leaders of fascist organizations," and Luca claimed that "Zionist organizations must be disbanded as enemies of the republic and treated as such."[24] Emil Bodnaras was pragmatic: "We lack housing; they [the emigrants] leave behind houses. We lack jobs for our youth; they leave behind jobs."[25]

In 1933 the Romanian Communist party had claimed 1,655 members, of which 364 were Jews. A Romanian researcher, Florian Banu, having consulted statistics concerning the ethnic origins of Romanian Communist party members, reports that in 1933 there were in fact 1,459 party members—375 Romanians, 444 Hungarians, 330 Jews, 140 Bulgarians, 100 Russians, and 70 Ukrainians.[26] Of these, the Jews represented 22.6 percent. Although Jews and non-Jews joined the party in massive numbers after 1945—for opportunistic reasons or out of political conviction—the actual percentage of Jews in the party dramatically decreased. In February 1946, for example, Jews represented only 5.3 percent of party members.

After surviving the war among a population that was an object of total discrimination, some Jews now became members of the Communist elite, both in the party and in the military. While they by no means dominated the party leadership (the Politburo and the Secretariat), a good many Jews could be found in the Central Committee and in the regional party bureaucracies. In 1949, Jews comprised fewer than 10 percent of the members of the Securitate, the secret police organization, yet their presence was proportionally greater in its leadership. Anti-Semites exploited this influence to create the impression that Jews dominated the secret police.[27]

More specifically, in 1948, when the Securitate was created, its employees had the following ethnic backgrounds:

Romanians	3,334 (83.9%)
Jews	338 (8.5%)
Hungarians	247 (6.2%)
Russians	24 (0.6%)
Yugoslavs	13 (0.3%)
Others	17 (0.4%)
Total	3,973[28]

Thus Jews were the most powerfully represented of the minority groups, yet in terms of sheer numbers they were no challenge to the Romanian contingent. Their numbers and consequent power were nonetheless magnified by political gossips for political ends.

In keeping with its long tradition of anti-Semitism, Romania blamed the Jews for the casualties and excesses of Communist rule, and for the government's harshly repressive tactics for dealing with dissidence. Yet Jews, not surprisingly, were appalled by the tactics of the regime. A 1946 CDE report identified six categories of "disgruntled" Jews: former deportees, former inmates at forced labor camps, orphans, the handicapped, war widows, and former tenants evacuated by Antonescu's state agency in charge of the Aryanization of Jewish properties.[29] From this grim situation, the Jews emigrated. Even the CDE acknowledged that racial discrimination and Zionist activities fueled the general exodus.[30]

The famine of 1946–1947 triggered a new wave of anti-Semitism, especially in Moldova. Jewish merchants were blamed for the increased cost of food, and their reserves were often raided and confiscated by the police. Florian Banu writes, "Naturally the question 'Where is the grain?' was raised, and the answer appeared: In Palestine, where it was sent by Ana Pauker. . . . The conviction that the Jews [were] responsible for the food situation of the country increased together with the shortages. . . . It is interesting to note that representatives of the democratic opposition, in their attempt to undermine the position of the Communists, did not hesitate to appeal to a sentiment which does not have anything to do with democracy: anti-Semitism."[31]

At the 1946 Paris Peace Conference, at which the Romanian delegation lied about the nation's role in the Holocaust, former prime minister and member of the new Communist regime Gheorghe Tatarescu had warned Rabbi Safran: "Do not forget that although we are now in Paris, we belong to Romania; do not forget that we shall leave Paris and return to Romania and meet there again."[32] Prime Minister Petru Groza, normally respectful of Rabbis Safran and Rosen, supported anti-Semitic measures. Groza and Rosen had remained in friendly contact through the most repressive years of the Stalinist era. Son of an Orthodox priest and a wealthy fellow traveler of the Romanian Communist party, Groza had even asked Rosen to conduct a service in Hebrew at his funeral. Safran said of Groza: "It is difficult to judge how serious he was . . . although he was prime minister, he had no real power. I knew well enough that the . . . matters I presented to him were not taken into

his office but into the one opposite, occupied by Emil Bodnaras, the general secretary of the Council of Ministers. If
I left Groza's office with promises that my requests regarding various matters (emigration, for instance) would be
solved, I knew that those promises had to be confirmed by
Bodnaras; his voice would carry great weight, especially regarding the matter of the Jews leaving Romania for the
Holy Land."[33]

Safran's assessment was accurate. Groza, though apparently pro-Jewish, was politically weak and sometimes hypocritical in reporting to the Romanian Communist party on
the emigration activities of the Jewish community. When it
came to Bodnaras, the real power behind the problem of
Jewish emigration, as Safran writes, he "never took an official stand regarding matters of principle as for instance the
Zionist doctrine. Being a very practical man he in fact
played a major role in solving the concrete problems of Jewish emigration. Actually solving the matter depended on
him directly, as he was all-powerful within the regime and
the Russians trusted him."[34]

In June 1949, Groza told Bodnaras, "Now the Americans are playing their Jewish card. And it's not at all difficult
to play that card in a country with 400,000 Jews, and with
tens of thousands of them infiltrating into our state, economic, political, and cultural apparatus. . . . It's full of Jews.
Everywhere you look there are Jews. How can you expect
the Jews working for instance in the State Planning Commission to carry out an honest and decent day's work . . .
[when they've] been placed in posts planning [the daily
functioning of] the very factories and commercial enterprises that were expropriated from them? The Zionists are
the perfect candidates for being the fifth column [in this

country]."[35] Political measures were soon advanced against the new enemy.

In 1949, Romanian Communists began a brutal campaign against the Zionists. Over the course of the next ten years, as Mihai Pelin, a Romanian historian, writes, some 250 Zionist leaders and low-ranking militants were arrested, interrogated under terrible conditions, and tried by military courts. "In the beginning it was obvious that a new public Zionist trial [was being] prepared. Stalin's death complicated things, but the communists did not give up. Measures against the Zionists continued."[36] Zionists were accused, Pelin writes, of "plotting against the regime; misleading the Jewish population, taking it to Israel in order to insure conscripts for the imperialists; collaboration with the reactionary forces against the working class; and espionage."[37] In July, Rabbi Zissu Portugal, a leader of the Agudath Israel and savior of the orphans from Transnistria, was arrested. Two months later, having received no explanation, he was released. In September 1950 the Romanian legation in Tel Aviv reported that former Alyah Beth Mossad Jewish parachutists were involved in "the campaign against Romania." According to diplomatic documents, the parachutists had in fact publicly protested the arrest of Zionists in Romania.[38]

Public exchanges between Israel and Communist countries soon grew increasingly divisive. During the trial of Rudolf Slansky in Czechoslovakia (on charges of traitorous activities), Radio Bucharest proclaimed, "We have criminals among us, Zionist agents and agents of international Jewish capitalism. We shall expose them, and it is our duty to exterminate them."[39]

On February 11, 1953, the Soviet Union ended diplomatic relations with Israel. Rabbi Portugal was again arrested and again released. In March 1954 a trial of Romanian Zionists began. With the support of government and public opinion, forty-eight people in Tel Aviv went on a hunger strike. In July a Romanian court condemned more than a hundred Jews for espionage. That same day in the Israeli parliament, Moshe Sharett protested: "The Israeli government finds unconvincing the declarations of the Romanian government on the basis of which over one hundred Jews have been condemned to long [prison] terms."[40]

As Jewish emigration grew into a highly political issue in both countries, the intelligence agencies of the respective governments became increasingly involved. In the late 1940s and early 1950s both Romanian and Israeli intelligence activities were reorganized. In August 1948 the Romanian Communist party established the Securitate. Two months earlier the Sherut Yediot (or, SHAI)—Hebrew for "Information Service"—had been created in Tel Aviv and placed under the supervision of Reuven Shiloah, special adviser to the prime minister. According to the historians Dan Raviv and Yossi Melman, SHAI included three elements: a domestic secret service, Shin Beth, led by Isser Harel; a foreign intelligence service, the so-called Political Department, led by Boris Guriel; and the Institute for Alyah Beth, in charge of emigration, led by Shaul Avigur.[41]

At a 1950 symposium in Israel, Shiloah declared: "We have not yet begun serious work in the states of Eastern Europe. We hope to do this in the future. There is a need to extend help to the [Israeli] missions dealing with the problems of the Jewish communities [in those countries] and the problems of immigration to Israel from those countries. We suffer from a lack of suitable people to do intelligence work abroad. Before the establishment of the state, we could rely on the help of loyal Jews and non-Jews in addition to special units of Haganah personnel from [Palestine]. This supportive and special attitude toward us has changed. . . . The minister must be a partner in intelligence matters. On the other hand, it is clear to the [Political] department that there is an urgent need for each mission to have one person whose job will be to deal only with intelligence matters."[42] Eliahu Epstein (Elath), Israel's minister in London, emphasized that some intelligence work could be handled above ground, especially in Western European countries where contacts with military and scientific circles were legal.[43]

Echoing Elath, Ehud Avriel, minister to Bucharest and former minister to Prague, clearly distinguished between the division's work in Western and Eastern Europe. In the East, influential and knowledgeable people could not be accessed, and Israeli diplomats were under constant counterintelligence surveillance. He suggested, therefore, that operatives in Eastern Europe focus their efforts on studying and foiling Soviet-bloc counterintelligence: "Who are the people following us? What means are they using? What does the Kominform know about the Jews?" Avriel continued, "It is important to know at least several hours in advance about impending actions against the Jews; it is important to know which people are betraying us, who is trying to sabotage our activities, etcetera. In these countries the ministers themselves must serve as intelligence agents. They have contacts. . . . In addition to the minister, there is room in each mission for a Political Department man. . . . The best cover is the commercial [attaché's] job, and it is best that whoever carries [the title] will be able to do the job properly."[44] Immediately after this meeting, Israeli intelligence was accordingly reorganized.[45]

Isser Harel, then head of Shin Beth, explained: "The Shin Beth's debriefing on recent immigrants from behind the Iron Curtain and the orderly transmission of the information collected—on Soviet industrial and military and other strategic installations—for the CIA seems to have begun in June or early July 1951."[46] The U.S. diplomatic mission in Israel was interested in this information as well as in news of the "persecution of religious dissidents, the denial of human rights behind the Iron Curtain, and forced labor camps." The American consulate provided this information by interviewing Jewish emigrants from the Eastern bloc and by consulting Romanian newspapers and journals as well as Israeli government press releases and official reports.[47]

Coordinated by the deputy head of the American consulate, Erwin P. Keeler, and by Steven Zakorski, a consular attaché, these information-gathering operations, known as Trevi and Peripheral Security, worried the Israelis. Shiloah and other Israeli leaders feared they might disrupt relations with Communist governments or jeopardize future arrangements for the emigration of Jews to Israel. Shiloah thus imposed strict limitations on cooperation with Trevi and Peripheral Security activities.[48]

Shiloah had good reason to be cautious. From its opening, the Israeli consulate in Bucharest had been infiltrated by Romanian secret service agents. Consequently, as Pelin writes, the Israeli consulate was "under extraordinary pressure, being under careful surveillance from outside and inside. In the private homes of Ehud Avriel, commercial attaché, and Eliezer Halevy, secretary of the legation, microphones were installed." Romanian agents, code named

Lagu, LT9, and G, reported on all the Israeli diplomats, while code name X specifically reported on Zvi Locker and Halevy. Zoltan Hirsch, alias LT9, was a prime Securitate agent at the Israeli consulate. He reported mainly to Ehud Avriel, the minister in Bucharest, but also to Eliezer Halevy, deputy chief of the mission. Hirsch's wife, Regina Fischler, a telephone operator for the Israeli legation, was also allegedly recruited by the Securitate.[49] Thus when it came to emigration matters, caution was a byword for the Israelis.

In August 1949 the Romanian Communist party secretariat reached a consensus on the emigration of the Jews. It would permit emigration and simultaneously intensify the propaganda against it by publishing letters from Palestine that described the "misery" there.[50] Levy and Pauker write, "A synthesis prepared . . . at the end of 1949 revealed that while only 400–500 Jews had been allowed to emigrate between January and September–October 1949, the number had increased to some 3,000–4,000 by the end of the year."[51]

Behind the sudden rush of emigrants was Israeli pressure. On October 1, Ben-Gurion met in Tel Aviv with Nicolae Cioroiu, the leading Romanian diplomat in Israel. Ben-Gurion told him that "the development of relations between the two countries depends on the evolution of the economic relations and on the emigration of the Jews who want to leave Romania."[52] A month later Moshe Sharett, Israel's foreign minister, protested to the same Cioroiu that the Romanian government was unfairly constraining Jewish emigration: Israeli ships were no longer permitted to call in Romania, collective departures were canceled, and severe restrictions made individual departures increasingly difficult. The meeting was tense. Sharett said to Cioroiu, "Immigration is the political axis of the government of Israel. The Jews from Romania are a determining factor in Israel. RPR [the Popular Republic of Romania], the enemy of Zionism and of [the Israeli] government, refuses [to meet for] discussions, did not answer our letter, attacks us, arrests Zionists, and does not respect the promises given to Namir and Agami. Eliasiv [director of the Israeli Foreign Ministry] is not received officially. . . . I cannot conceive [of] diplomatic relations between two states with [such] completely opposed views, especially concerning emigration."[53]

Sharett's words were not empty threats. On November 21, 1949, Israel recalled Rubin and Agami from Romania. Israeli newspapers launched a massive press campaign against the Romanian authorities. Israeli officials were unhappy with Rubin's results in promoting Jewish emigration; by withdrawing the veteran Agami, Israel demonstrated its skepticism about the future of emigration from Romania.

Yet Israel could not long ignore the importance of Romania's Jewish population. Two months after Agami and Rubin's departure, Israel nominated Avriel to head the Israeli consulate in Bucharest. The Israeli government continued to entreat Romania to let the Jews go. But as diplomatic efforts continued to fail, Israel turned to less conventional means.

In November 1949, Zalman Robinson, a Romanian Jew, arrived in the Romanian port of Constanta. A civilian there gave him money and directed him to the train station. When he reached Bucharest, a car took him directly to Ana Pauker's house. Robinson was Pauker's brother. Unlike Ana, who had become a full member of the Romanian Communist party's Politburo as well as a foreign minister, Zalman

Robinson had remained an Orthodox Jew.[54] He had emigrated to Palestine in 1944 and was returning in 1949 to visit his sister. He stayed with Pauker in the very house in which she met fellow members of the Politburo.

As Moses Rosen later recalled, "No two people could have held more different views than Zalman and Ana—he was deeply religious and a staunch Zionist; she was a convinced Communist and an atheist. Yet they had a profound love and respect for each other. They recognized that in their different ways they were idealists. When Zalman first came to her house, Ana embraced and kissed him and said to him in Yiddish, 'Zalman, you have come home.' To this he replied, 'Home is Israel, not here.'"[55] In Bucharest, Robinson continued his pious life, kept in touch with his fellow Orthodox Jews and with the Israeli legation in Bucharest, and taught Jewish children Hebrew and Talmud at the synagogue.

Leibovici-Lais, a personal friend of Zalman Robinson, reported that a senior official in the Israeli government had approached Robinson shortly before he left for Romania and asked him to speak with his sister about Jewish emigration. Likewise Israel's foreign ministry contacted Robinson's wife, Dina, just before she left for Romania, and told her that her husband, as Pauker's brother, "should personally work on emigration problems."[56] The Israeli government and the Israeli legation in Bucharest, having exhausted their patience with traditional forms of diplomacy, came to rely increasingly on the personal influence of Zalman Robinson.

Although Robinson was sometimes a superfluous contact—by the spring of 1950, Jews in Romania could openly emigrate to Israel—the legation nevertheless persuaded him to stay in the country. When the emigration tide turned again that summer, and restrictions were renewed, the Israelis again relied on Robinson, dubbed by Ben-Gurion "the empress' brother."

From the outset, Robinson exploited every opportunity and occasion to intervene with his sister. He appealed to her "countless times . . . to allow free emigration . . . particularly for Zionist Jews." Beginning in December 1949 he exhorted her to allow Zionists, especially religious Zionists, to emigrate, arguing that religious Jews and Zionists should be allowed to leave "since they were not well regarded in Romania."[57] In addition to these constant appeals to his sister to ease Jewish emigration, Robinson actively sought the release of arrested Zionists. He also pressured his sister to allow medicine to be sent into prisons for those Jews who were sick.[58]

Robinson was a man of courage. Rosen writes, "When the Romanian authorities arrested the Zionist leadership on July 10, 1950, Zalman was outraged. He heard that the Romanian leaders, whom he knew well, as he had met them at his sister's house, were having a meeting with her. He burst into the room where they were assembled, holding a piece of paper. The startled leaders asked him what he wanted. 'I have a written request,' he replied. 'You have arrested the heads of the Zionist organizations. I am a Zionist. Please arrest me, too.' The Communist leaders burst out laughing. They found his intervention highly amusing and even tried to exchange jokes with him."[59]

When Ana Pauker fell from power in June 1952, emigration to Israel came to a standstill. During her tenure no fewer than 100,000 Jews had left Romania to settle in Israel. Yet, as Rosen writes, "she was a passionate, convinced Communist, who totally rejected the Zionists' thesis on the existence of a Jewish nation whose country was Israel. She strenuously argued that Romanian Jews were Romanian nationals whose duty it was to build up their Romanian homeland together with the Romanian masses. . . . Was she influenced by her Zionist brother Zalman, to allow Jews to leave for Israel? . . . Though unlikely, this notion cannot be ruled out. Was she influenced by the Holocaust, realizing the fate that might await those who remained in the Diaspora?"[60]

Even today, with the power of hindsight, Rosen's questions cannot be unequivocally answered. Robinson, regarded by the Rabbi of Buhusi as "our telephone to the Kominform" and by Rosen as a "saintly but naive man," was arrested on April 30, 1953. He spent two and a half years in a Romanian prison. He returned to Israel devastated, according to Rosen, after one of his daughters attempted to commit suicide, believing that Ana had fallen from power because of him.[61]

Israel's attempts to ease the emigration of Romanian Jews did not prove fruitless. On November 29, 1949, the Romanian Ministry of the Interior cautiously relaxed its emigration criteria, allowing more Jews—with the exception of technicians—to emigrate. But departures were granted individually in order to avoid a disruption of Romania's economy.[62] According to archival records, "Departures jumped from 100 to between 500 and 600 a month in the last part of 1949, and increased to roughly 2,500 per month at the beginning of 1950—with a total of 15,500 people leaving for Israel between November 1949 and April 1950 when the gates suddenly opened completely. On March 31, 1950, the Interior Ministry [under the leadership of Politburo member Georgescu] met to discuss the party's decision to issue 10,000 to 12,000 exit visas per month be-

ginning in April 1950. . . . The numbers rapidly exceeded all
expectations, as from January 1 to June 1, 1950, some
47,000 people received exit visas, 37,000 of them in April
and May alone."[63] Between January 1 and May 15, 1950,
53,480 emigration requests were submitted.[64] By the following June, the Romanian Ministry of the Interior was determining how much each Jewish emigrant would be
allowed to take with him.

Romania's relaxed emigration policies prompted a Jewish exodus. From the eleventh district in Bucharest alone,
12,200 Jews registered to leave. By May 12, 1950, 6,146
Jews from Bacau had registered, and 6,500 of the 10,000
Jews in Arad (of which 600 were Communist party members). Sometimes the local police went door to door to distribute emigration forms, and in Saveni, Moldova, they beat
drums to announce to the Jews that forms for departure
were available to be picked up.

A CDE report on Jewish emigration for the year 1950
contains the following numbers:

January	1,500
February	2,000
March	3,000
April	3,000
May	4,000
June	5,000
July	7,000
August	7,000
September	7,000
October	4,000
November	3,000
December	3,000[65]

The exodus continued in 1951, as 50,000 to 60,000 Jews received exit visas. By the time the Romanian Communist party ended this free flow, exit visas had been issued to 100,000 Jews.[66]

The general Romanian population showed mixed feelings about this exodus. In Moldova, Romanian factory workers expressed sympathy for the emigrants, saying that the Jews had relatives in Israel who missed them, and that life would be better for them there. In Botosani, a non-Jewish female member of the Communist Youth (UTM) said of the emigration: "This is treason, they all must be hanged." A young Jewish woman and member of the same organization replied: "This is exactly why we need to leave; you will have nobody to hang." The employees of a Tarnaveni textile store hung their sentiments on a poster in the window: Jewish customers were not welcome. Georgescu, president of the co-op union in Radauti, when entreated by a sick Jew for a car to go to the hospital, answered, "When you went to Transnistria, were you given a car?"[67]

Those who hoped to emigrate found that economic and financial contributions to the Romanian Communist party were advisable. Agami's recently declassified memoirs indicate that until 1947 "[our] relationship [to] the regime's leadership was not based on bribery."[68] But new considerations soon applied.

Despite the new emigration criteria adopted in 1948 and 1949, Romanian Communist authorities continued to see emigration as an important source of income. Andrew and Leslie Cockburn write that "Though the Kremlin had endorsed the principle of free emigration, local governments were given latitude in extracting whatever price they could either for the state treasury desperate for hard currency or for officials eager to replenish their personal incomes."[69] In Israel, Ben-Gurion grumbled in his diary about Romania, "You can't do anything without money. From top to bottom, even the Communist [party] wants money."[70]

In the fall of 1949, according to an agreement between the Israeli legation in Bucharest and Sovromtransport, a Romanian-Russian transport service largely under Russian control, the legation was obliged to pay $57 for every third-class ticket on a ship bound from Romania to Israel.[71] In December, when Rubin's mission in Romania was brought to an end, Pauker told him that the legation's contribution toward the emigration was inadequate. Once back in Israel, Rubin proposed raising the emigrant fee to $120, under the condition that Romania release 50,000 Jews.[72] A meeting in June 1950 between Sovromtransport, the Israeli consul, and Deputy Chief of Mission Halevy established that the Israeli consulate would pay $90 for each of the 1,300 tickets on the ship *Transylvania*, the sole vessel designated by Romanian authorities for emigration to Israel.[73] But the established fee was not what was in fact paid. Israeli intelligence experts Melman and Raviv have confirmed that Romanian authorities were paid $100 for each passenger.[74]

According to a 1951 government report, Romania had come to depend on this important source of hard currency: "It is difficult for the [Romanian] state, at this point, to renounce a yearly income in hard currency of about two million."[75]

Israelis were willing to pay not just for travel expenses but also for the right of Jews to emigrate. In 1949, with the help of Ephraim Illin, the Israeli businessman earlier involved in the Czech-Israeli arms deal, Shaike Dan helped create an Israeli-Yugoslav company which, according to

Amos Ettinger, gave Yugoslavia a $200,000 steel-making furnace manufactured by the Brassard Brothers, twelve oil-drilling installations, and eight American-manufactured luxury cars for Yugoslavian leaders, products they could not buy direct from the West. Dan was thus returning the favors extended to him during the transit of the Romanian Jews via Yugoslavia.[76]

Yugoslavia was not the only Communist country interested in drilling equipment. Before the Arab oil boom, Romania had been one of the world's major oil producers. From the turn of the century, American oil companies, chiefly New Jersey's Standard Oil, had invested heavily there.[77] In 1938, Standard-owned Romano-Americana was the fourth-largest oil company in Romania. That year U.S. investment comprised 10 percent of the Romanian oil industry.

In 1938, Nazi Germany, preparing for its campaign on the Eastern Front, began seizing U.S. and British oil operations in Romania.[78] Antonescu's empowerment ensured their success. During World War II the Allied forces naturally sought to disrupt Romanian oil production in order to harass Germany's war effort. In 1945 the Soviets took possession of the Romanian oil fields and transported much of the oil-drilling equipment to the Soviet Union as war trophy. Washington and London protested, maintaining that the equipment belonged to British and American oil companies and had been taken illegally by the Germans.[79] By March 1945 the Romano-Americana oil company was complaining that the Soviets had carried away 65 percent of its equipment. Against these charges, the Soviets maintained that all the equipment they seized bore German markings, had not been paid for by Romano-Americana, and was destined for the Baku oil fields. The U.S. State Department's reply was brief: Return our equipment or pay for it.[80] Between 1945 and 1947 a Soviet-American commission in Bucharest discussed the removal of oil equipment from Romania to little effect.[81]

The Soviet seizure of their oil-drilling resources left Romanian authorities desperate. In 1947, with the support of the Lehman Brothers, Nicolae Malaxa, a Romanian industrialist, traveled to the United States, where, for $8 million, he contracted with the International Derrick and Equipment Company to supply oil-drilling equipment to Romania.[82] Soon after, Romania became a Communist dictatorship, and Washington annulled the deal.

Like the Yugoslavs, the Romanians sought to rehabilitate their oil industry from the ravages of the war. As Dan recalled, "This kind of equipment could only be had in the West, and it seems [the Romanians] knew who to turn to. . . . I took my expert Ephraim Illin, and we left for Bucharest as guests of the Romanian trade ministry. . . . The talks with the Romanians were all business and straight to the point. Three or four drilling instruments weren't enough for them. They wanted a whole boatload and were ready to pay in full. . . . Unlike the Yugoslavs, they also intended to get paid for issuing exit permits to the Jews. Ever since the *Pan York* and the *Pan Crescent*, no Jews had left Romania. Now we were in a good bargaining position. Ephraim Illin took care of the business side and I of the Jewish side."[83]

According to Leibovici-Lais, negotiations on the oil-drilling equipment began in January 1949, with Namir and Pauker at the helm, and continued in 1950 with Illin and Dan. Pauker asked Namir to delegate the details of the negotiations to Agami and her deputy Ana Toma.[84]

Informed of Pauker's request, Moshe Sharett, the Israeli foreign minister, immediatelly sent Agami to Bucharest as an Israeli diplomat. But his negotiations with the Romanian authorities went nowhere. So, with the help of Avriel and Dan, Agami contacted Illin. They met in Paris, and Illin gladly provided the Romanians with oil-drilling equipment, pipe, and tractors in exchange for Jews.

Israel held mixed feelings about the deal, especially since it might break the U.S. embargo against Romania. As Illin recalled, "Bitter disputes broke out among us regarding the question of whether we had the right and the ability to risk acting in opposition to American policy. Reuven Shiloah, one of the key men in the Foreign Office, was firmly opposed to the deal. Ehud Avriel, Shaike Dan, Shaul Avigur, Yosef Bartel, and, of course, Moshe Agami were in favor. I declared that we had no choice but to act in accordance with our own best interests. It was not a matter of some small smuggling operation but of a political act that we owed to ourselves, to the Holocaust survivors, and to those who did not have the protection of the Jewish state and were massacred by the Nazis. After much discussion and wavering, the decision was made and I was given the go-ahead."[85]

Anticipating that the deal might not go through, or that it might be leaked, Shiloah prepared for possible failure. He sent a coded cable to the Israeli legation in Bucharest, stating, as Illin recalls: "Illin is going to Romania, thinking that he will solve the immigration problem. We have no basis to believe that he will succeed. Do not identify with him, do not cooperate with him, avoid all direct contact with him. If he does succeed, he will be congratulated. If he fails, do not give him any help."[86])

Illin thought at first that the Romanian deal was a "replay of the Yugoslavian script." Yet he soon realized that this was an "entirely different opera. . . . The Yugoslavians—if one may make a generalization about national character—are frank and at times even naive. . . . The Romanians were absolutely different: suspicious, troublemaking, quarrelsome, and petty. Negotiations with them were as difficult as parting the Red Sea, particularly when they were represented by Jewish Communists—a curse not recorded in the Torah. Although the Yugoslavians were also dedicated Communists, they were patriots first and foremost, always bearing in mind what was best for Yugoslavia. [Romania] . . . was an extremist Communist country."[87]

Negotiating with Gogu Radulescu, the Romanian minister of foreign trade, his deputy Abramowitz, and a Russian security agent proved challenging. A deal was nevertheless reached and implemented: the Romanians paid for the oil-drilling equipment partly in cash and partly in Jews. As Dan recalled, "The instruments and the drill pipes were at that time more important to the Romanians than a few more Jews. . . . The agreement signed between Ephraim Illin and the Romanians dealt with a whole shipload of drilling equipment. Even though no mention was made of a quid pro quo, the agreement between me and the Romanians spoke about exit permits for many thousands of Jews still in Romania. The figure was astronomical, about 20 percent of all the Jews still in Romania, but the Romanians gladly agreed."[88]

Both sides benefited from the arrangement. Israel received nearly 100,000 new citizens from Romania over the course of two years, and Romania's economy was buoyed by the influx of fresh currency and oil-drilling equipment.

4

Barter

World War II and poor postwar management devastated Romania's economy. The new Romanian Communist regime introduced ill-advised economic measures, including the nationalization of industries, land, and real estate, and tight control of hard currency; the Soviet Union imposed heavy war reparations on Romania for its role in the occupation of part of the Ukraine; and the cold war ruled out economic support from the West. Together, America's export regulations and Romania's socialization decrees dramatically reduced Romanian-American trade. In 1950 U.S. exports to Romania amounted to $1.5 million dollars; in the same year Romania's exports to the United States were a mere $150,000.[1]

Diplomatic relations between the United States and Romania reached their nadir in the late 1940s and early 1950s. U.S. diplomatic personnel were systematically harassed in Bucharest. In September 1948, four members of the American consulate, charged with taking photographs in a forbidden zone, were detained for sixteen hours. Romanian authorities asked Washington to recall two of its diplomats, and American officials acquiesced. Between 1949 and 1951, Romanian officials forced the United States to reduce from fifty-three to eleven the staff of its consulate in Bucharest, and enforced travel restrictions on those who remained: they had to stay within seventy miles of the city. The Romanian government closed U.S. and British libraries and arrested and tried their employees, and harassed journalists as well.

Romanian officials claimed that Washington treated their country with undeserved disfavor, and that diplomatic relations between the two countries had decayed due to unfair U.S. policies rather than injustices committed by the Romanian government.[2] As the historians Joseph Harrington and Bruce Courtney describe the situation, "During the last two months of 1951, harassment [by Romanian officials] increased. . . . While Romania's behavior toward the American legation was in part due to Soviet pressure, the harassment was also a direct reaction to several aspects of America's policy toward Eastern Europe. Bucharest was especially disturbed by Washington's continued protests concerning Romania's human rights violations. . . . Further, Romania objected to America's unwillingness to export needed industrial products to Romania."[3]

Despite Romania's complaints, the State Department continued to protest its human rights violations. On August 1, 1951, President Truman suspended Romania's Most Favored Nation (MFN) trade status.[4] By 1952 Romanian harassment and American trade restrictions had almost rendered defunct the U.S. consulate in Bucharest; there was even talk of closing it altogether.[5]

In March that year Romanian authorities nearly halted Jewish emigration from Romania to Israel. The *Transylvania*, which sailed from Constanta to the Israeli port of

Haifa, had provided the principal mode of transportation. Romanian authorities docked the ship ostensibly for repairs, and provided no substitute vessel.[6] In 1952, 3,712 Romanian Jews emigrated to Israel; between 1953 and 1954 this number dropped to several dozen; between 1953 and 1958, despite U.S. condemnation, a mere 1,657 Jews emigrated.

Stalin's death in 1953 did nothing to diminish Romania's anti-Semitic policies. Jewish emigration continued to be banned; more Zionists were arrested and tried, and in April 1954 two hundred were imprisoned, their sentences ranging from fifteen years to life.[7]

For Israel, Jewish emigration—and not only from Romania—remained a priority. In 1952, Shaul Avigur and Shaike Dan created the Liaison Bureau (known as the Lishka) in Israel to arrange Jewish emigration from the Soviet Union and Eastern Europe.[8] Run by Shaul Avigur, the bureau answered to Prime Minister Moshe Sharett and to the Ministry of Foreign Affairs. Based in Tel Aviv, not in Jerusalem with the Ministry of Foreign Affairs, the Liaison Bureau was parallel to the Mossad and Shin Beth in the structure of the Israeli intelligence community. Although it never had more than fifty people on staff, its role in coordinating the emigration of Jews to Israel was crucial. The fact that Shaul Avigur, "the grey eminence of Israel" and "an institution by himself," was in charge of this office for many years is telling in terms of its importance in the Israeli bureaucracy.[9]

Despite constraints imposed by Romanian authorities on the U.S. consulate in Bucharest, Washington did not lose interest in Romania. By using economic sanctions, the United States believed it could generate dissent between Moscow and her satellites.[10] The National Security Council (NSC) recommended that the U.S. government support nationalistic movements in the Soviet satellites, hoping that these movements might undermine Soviet control and return Romania, as Harrington and Courtney write, to "the family of free and democratic nations."[11]

Washington was well aware of the challenges this policy posed. As the *New York Times* aptly commented, "No people dislike Communism more than the Romanians, and none do less against it."[12] In July 1956 the NSC reaffirmed America's goal to free the satellite states from Soviet control. Despite its historically Western orientation and the people's "Russophobia," Romania was viewed by the NSC as the satellite least likely to obtain its independence from Russia because it lacked a popular movement for change that could seriously challenge the local authorities. Regardless, Romania continued to press the West in general and especially the United States for trade development as well as for greater cultural exchanges.[13] Neither Washington nor London was receptive.[14]

Emil Bodnaras, worried about the state of Romanian diplomatic and trade relations with the West, tried to use the Romanian Jewish community, and especially Rosen, to improve his country's image in the eyes of the international community. In 1955, under heavy surveillance, Bodnaras permitted Rosen to attend the World Peace Assembly in Helsinki and later to confer with Chief Rabbi Kurt Wilhelm of Sweden at conferences in Romania and in Sweden.

During 1955 and 1956, according to Rosen, Bodnaras remained circumspectly supportive of Jewish emigration. "It was he who, with caution and able tactics, regularly backed my efforts to resume *alyah*. It was due to him that I was able to travel abroad and establish bridges with our Jewish brethren."[15] Before leaving for Stockholm, Rosen asked Bodnaras for passports for A. L. Zissu and Misu Ben-evenisti, Zionist leaders whom the Communist authorities had recently freed from prison. Bodnaras granted the passports, but when Rosen asked Bodnaras for two hundred additional passports for other Zionist activists, Bodnaras hesitated. "If your trip is a success," he said—by which he meant the appropriate contacts and statements, and Rosen's return home—"your requests will be granted."[16]

Despite Rosen's minor successes and Bodnaras's conditional generosity, Israeli diplomats continued to view the condemned Zionists in Romania and the emigration of the Jews as chief priorities. With emigration from Eastern Europe to Israel having come almost to a standstill, future prospects appeared bleak. Between January and April 1956, just eighty-two Jews emigrated from Eastern Europe to Israel: twenty-three from Hungary, fifteen from the Soviet Union, fourteen from Bulgaria, five from Czechoslovakia, and twenty-five from Romania. Golda Meir, the Israeli foreign minister, confronted Gheorghe Chitic, the Romanian chargé d'affaires in Tel Aviv, about emigration.[17] And Israeli diplomatic envoys to Romania, visiting or stationed in Bucharest, continued to press Romanian authorities to increase the pace of Jewish emigration.[18]

Bilateral discussions on the issue of the "reunification of the families" (a Romanian euphemism for emigration) almost always led to trade or commercial negotiations. To promote these transactions, the Romanian Ministry of Foreign Affairs asked Chitic to be amenable during negotiations with his Israeli counterparts.

In November 1956, Elkanah Margalit, an Israeli diplomat in Bucharest, asked the Romanian deputy minister of foreign affairs to try to persuade Egypt to enter into direct peace negotiations with Israel. This was Romania's first opportunity to mediate in the Middle East conflict. In the same year the Federation of the Romanian Jewish Communities was granted approval to publish a magazine in Romanian, Hebrew, and Yiddish (English was added later), a few hundred copies of which were also to be distributed in the Soviet Union. These timid overtures did not preclude the Romanian authorities from pressing Chief Rabbi Moses Rosen to condemn Israel as the aggressor in the 1956 Suez War. Meanwhile Romania played the Soviet game with servility as Bodnaras and other Romanian Communist leaders supported the Russian intervention in Hungary.

In August 1957 the Romanian consulate in Tel Aviv communicated to Israeli authorities that of the 180 Zionists arrested in Romania, 179 had been freed. Romania now wished to discuss the reunification of the families, but not *alyah*. On September 12, according to diplomatic documents, Israeli president Yitzhak Ben-Zvi lunched with Romania's leading diplomat in Jerusalem; the president reiterated the problem of reunification.[19] Roughly two months later the leading Israeli diplomat in Bucharest, Arie Harell, gave Prime Minister Chivu Stoica a letter from Ben-Gurion in which the Israeli prime minister emphasized the humanitarian aspects of Jewish emigration to Israel, criticized the slow rate at which it had recently proceeded, and appealed to the Romanian government to find an "administrative solution" to accelerate matters. Stoica replied—by letter to Ben-Gurion and verbally to Harell—that "the Romanian government is carefully following the problem of reunification of the families. . . . The Romanian government will not allow mass emigration [because] this issue is a strictly internal one."[20]

A report by the American embassy in Bucharest concluded that the years 1955 and 1956 represented a period of
relative stability for Romanian Jews. "Those who remained
wished to leave but were cautious to show it, because those
who intended this were discredited through quasi-repressive
measures. The emigration process ended almost totally."[21]
The report noted that, while there were few official signs of
anti-Semitism, it was nonetheless widespread in the Romanian population. Not only were Jews perceived as having
taken advantage of the Communist regime, but Romanians
generally believed that Jews were unfaithful to the regime.
"All arguments [that] served to denigrate the Jews were useful even if they contradicted what actually was the case."
After the Hungarian revolution, Romanian authorities began to apply a policy of *numerus clausus*—a quota system—
which systematically eliminated Jews from government
positions. "Discreet and confidential" at the start, it became
increasingly obvious.[22]

Suddenly, however, Romanian emigration policy
shifted. On May 31, 1958, at a meeting of the Romanian
Communist party Politburo, members were presented with
a report of roughly 37,000 unprocessed emigration requests: 26,302 Jews asked to go to Israel, 8,426 to the Fed-
eral Republic of Germany, and 2,088 to Austria, Canada,
and the United States. Gheorghiu-Dej approved in principle the emigration of all these people, saying it should take
place "gradually."[23] Around the same time, Soviet troops
withdrew from Romania.

Bodnaras crucially influenced this change of policy. According to Harrington and Courtney, "[Roughly two years]
after Stalin's death in March 1953, Nikita Khrushchev visited
Bucharest. While there he met an 'old Bolshevik' comrade,

Emil Bodnaras, the Romanian defense minister. During their conversation, according to Khrushchev, Bodnaras raised the question, 'What would you think about pulling your troops out of Romania?' Khrushchev admitted to being taken aback by the question and made the rather elusive response that the Soviet Union had to keep troops stationed in Romania because of a possible Turkish offensive."[24] Khrushchev, at any rate, lost his temper, and the Romanians withdrew the request.[25] In 1958 Bodnaras again approached Khrushchev on the subject. By that time the Hungarian revolution had dramatically improved Khrushchev's opinion of the Romanian Communist party and Bodnaras's credentials. The historian Sergiu Verona writes, "Romania's behavior proved faultless during the Soviet intervention in Hungary," and Bodnaras was the "key person in the Romanian leadership's support of the Soviets during the 1956 Hungarian uprising. Bodnaras was appointed minister of transport and communications when the transit of Soviet troops through Romania was essential to the USSR; he also played a key role in the arrangements for [Prime Minister] Imre Nagy's lodging [read arrest] in Romania after the Soviets abducted Nagy from Hungary."[26] Because Romania helped crush the Hungarian revolt, or because Romania was surrounded by Communist countries and was therefore of little strategic interest to the Red Army, or perhaps as a goodwill gesture by the USSR to the West, the Soviet army withdrew from Romania.

Shortly after this withdrawal, the Romanian Communist party began to shift the trajectory of Romania's trade away from the Soviet bloc.[27] In an interview with the *Washington Post*, Prime Minister Stoica indicated that Romania was willing to trade with the West. Washington remained unenthusiastic.[28]

The new relaxation of emigration restrictions for the Jews was undoubtedly linked by Romanian authorities to their hopes for trade with the West. Romanian Jews leaped at the chance to emigrate to Israel.[29] As Rosen observes, "When Romanian Jews heard on Yom Kippur 1958 that they could register for emigration to Israel, the effect on them was electrifying. So overwhelming was the feeling of joy, excitement, and relief that even ultra-orthodox Jews in Szatmar took off their *tallitoth*, put down their prayer books, left the synagogues, and began to queue up at police stations for exit permits. These dramatic scenes were repeated all over the country. Every day thousands of Jews gathered in Bucharest outside the central police station. The queues stretched for miles. It was an awesome sight. . . . The scenes were reminiscent of Messianic times."[30]

The American consulate in Bucharest reported on the Romanian Communist party's response: "During the months of October–December 1958, the police prefectures were literally under assault from 100,000 Jews who decided to leave the country. This action was perceived by the regime as a slap in the face (although it encouraged it under the slogan of 'family reunification'), and official anti-Semitism ceased to be discreet and became a drastic repression against the 'traitors.' All those who asked to emigrate were fired or severely demoted; students were expelled from universities. Gradually these measures were extended to those who did not ask to emigrate and whole areas such as the ministries of foreign affairs, defense, [and] foreign trade became Judenrein [free of Jews]."[31]

Israeli authorities were naturally pleased by this new *alyah*. Yet for Romanian authorities the new emigration policies created unexpected problems. In September 1958,

O-Farid El Chahlaoui, the United Arab Republic's ambassador to Bucharest, met with Vasile Dumitrescu, deputy minister of foreign affairs, to protest the emigration of Romanian Jews to Israel. In April 1959 the Egyptian newspapers *Al-Ahram* and *Le Progrès Egyptien* launched a press campaign against the same emigration. And the Lebanese government chimed in.[32] According to Leibovici-Lais, Arab ambassadors threatened to leave Bucharest. And when an office of the Keren-Hayesod (the equivalent of America's United Jewish Appeal) campaign was opened in Israel, Ben-Gurion denounced Romania for bowing to Arab pressures.[33]

Ben-Gurion's condemnation generated a fierce response from the newspaper of the Romanian Communist party. On February 25, 1959, *Scinteia* devoted its front page to an attack on Zionism. According to Rosen, it was an attack unseen in a major Romanian newspaper since the days of Lavrenty Beria. Worse was to come. The following day the government announced that the emigration of Jews to Israel was suspended. Thousands of exit permits, already issued, were canceled. Hundreds of Zionists were taken into custody. Young Jews were expelled from schools and universities.[34] The onslaught continued for several months. In the spring, Rabbi Portugal, the leader of the shattered Agudath Israel, was again arrested along with several hundred Jews suspected of being Zionist activists.[35] The West was outraged. Eleanor Roosevelt wrote to Romanian authorities to demand the release of three Jewish families.

Five days after the *Scinteia* article, an insulted and fearful Rosen met again with President Ion Gheorghe Maurer (they had met some five months earlier) to discuss Jewish emigration. Maurer told Rosen, "We know perfectly well who Rabbi Portugal is. . . . We the leadership, and not some police officer, decided that he should be arrested. We have thought the whole thing through. The fact that we took the decision to arrest him also means that we have considered the risks."[36] Maurer was furious: "Yes, Chief Rabbi, we wished to end our Jewish problem. I personally did not wish to feel like a prison administrator who cannot travel abroad for fear of being attacked and accused of holding innocent people in prison. My colleagues and I therefore hit on the idea of starting the registration of Jews to find out how many of them really wanted to leave. We expected 10,000 to 20,000 applications, but we received 130,000. Yes, 130,000. Who could have imagined such a figure? What terrible harm have we done to the Jewish people that they wish to leave in such huge numbers? We saved your lives, we granted you equal rights. Why should there be such a flight, worse than when the Jews were under the Fascists?"[37]

Maurer then explained further: "Nasser's ambassador comes to us and protests against the departure of the Romanian Jews, claiming that we are sending soldiers to Israel. We reply that this is not true, that only the old and handicapped are leaving. The ambassador then says to us, 'Whom should I believe, you or Ben-Gurion and Golda Meir?' Every evening they broadcast precise details of how many Romanian Jewish engineers, doctors, and young professionals have arrived in Israel. . . . We opened the gates of our country, so we should no longer be described in the world press as bandits. But our gesture has made no difference. Nothing has changed. We are still attacked and described as bandits. Well, if we are bandits when we keep the gates closed and bandits when we open them, we would rather keep them closed and avoid the problems we have with the Arabs."[38]

In response to the humiliation that Romanian authorities had suffered, and in exchange for its willingness to permit *alyah*, Maurer wanted the Israeli press to treat Romania more favorably. Israeli authorities agreed. According to Leibovici-Lais, Golda Meir met with representatives of the Israeli press and asked them to be discreet about the emigration of Romanian Jews to Israel. With the exception of *Haaretz*, the media complied, censoring themselves in order to avoid another scandal that would interrupt the emigration.[39] A few months later the emigration of Jews to Israel was resumed. Although it was not an exodus, the gates had opened once again. "But no one wrote about the *alyah* or spoke about it on radio or television," Rosen writes. "The Knesset made it an offense to refer to the arrival of the Romanian Jews by passing a special law. This emigration law acquired a special name, the *sha-sha alyah* (hush-hush *alyah*)."[40]

As their political and economic relations with the USSR proved fruitless, Romanian authorities desperately sought favorable trade relations with the West. In mid-April 1959, Romania notified Washington that it was willing to discuss war damage and the nationalization of U.S. interests.[41] Within two months Romania had secured $60 million in contracts with various Western companies.[42]

But Khrushchev had other plans for Romania, as part of an economic association for Communist Eastern Europe called Comecon. He wanted Romania to supply agricultural products and raw materials to the more industrially advanced countries of the Soviet bloc. Romania's leader Gheorghe Gheorghiu-Dej vehemently opposed Khrushchev's plan; he saw Romania as a future industrial center. Consequently "Romanian-Soviet trade soon slowed to a trickle."[43] The Sino-Soviet split, which Khrushchev announced at the 1960 party congress, and the 1962 Cuban missile crisis, provided Gheorghiu-Dej with sufficient room to pursue his own plans without risking a complete break with Moscow. At a Comecon meeting in February 1963, Romania declared that it would not modify its industrialization program. Gheorghiu-Dej and Tito now established a rapprochement, and in 1964 the Romanian Communist party issued the so-called April Declaration, which rejected the Soviet Union's rule of the Communist bloc and affirmed Romania's autonomy. At home, Gheorghiu-Dej ordered "de-Russification" and nationalistic "Romanization" measures to encourage general support for his defiance of Moscow and to deflect criticism from his own severe domestic economic policies. As cultural exchanges with the West multiplied and the jamming of foreign radio broadcasts ceased, Romania began opposing the Soviet Union in United Nations votes.[44]

Meanwhile Romanian authorities were using every possible means to improve their image in the West. In November 1961 they allowed Rabbi Rosen to travel to the United States. Rosen again sought to make himself indispensable to Romanian and Israeli authorities so that he could maintain a semblance of control over Jewish emigration to Israel.[45] In an interview with the *New York Times* during his stay in the United States, he praised Romania for permitting freedom of religion. Israeli authorities were not pleased. Golda Meir met Rosen in New York and told him, "The Romanian government should award you a special decoration for the services you have rendered them and for the speeches you are

making on their behalf in the United States. . . . You are dis-
rupting everything. I have come here to save the hungry and
persecuted Jews, but I find that you are proclaiming that life
is good in Romania. Is this not sabotaging our work?"[46] As
a result of this conversation, the Israeli consul in New York,
Meir Rosenne, strongly discouraged Rosen from visiting
Israel.

The vexation of Israeli officials was not confined to
Rosen. They were generally irritated by Romanian authorities who continued to harass Israeli diplomats stationed in
Bucharest. According to a September 1960 report by the
Romanian Ministry of Foreign Affairs, Israeli minister Ben-
dor participated "without being invited" in a commemora-
tion of the Iasi pogrom. The report also mentions that
between 1958 and 1960, Romanian authorities declared
four Israeli diplomats *persona non grata*. They also attempted to confine Israeli diplomats in Bucharest to one
synagogue in order to make surveillance easier and limit
their contact with Jewish parishioners. And though Romania professed an "anti-fascist" ideology, it refused to cooperate with Israel in the investigation of the case against
Adolf Eichmann.[47]

Romania's struggle for independence from the Soviet
Union did not go unnoticed in Washington. In a speech on
June 26, 1963, at the Free University of Berlin, President
Kennedy observed with favor Romania's "economic and political variation and dissent" vis-à-vis the Soviet bloc.[48] Taking advantage of Romania's increasing independence and its
consequent need for economic support, Washington promised better relations with Romania if its authorities could
speed the emigration of Jews. On August 7, William Craw-
ford, head of the U.S. legation in Bucharest, told Mircea

Malita, the Romanian deputy minister of foreign affairs, that "Romanian-American relations could best be improved were Bucharest to let more people emigrate, especially those seeking family reunification."[49]

Romanian authorities found themselves caught between the urgings of the United States and Israel to increase emigration and the Arab desire to shut it down. Objections were strongly put forward by the United Arab Republic's ambassador in Bucharest, and Romanian diplomats met with pressure at the ministries of foreign affairs in Baghdad and Damascus.[50]

U.S. foreign policy toward the Soviet Union's East European satellites remained consistent into the 1960s. In early 1964, Dean Rusk told the Senate Foreign Relations Committee that America's policy toward the Communist world had three objectives: "to prevent communism from expanding; to reduce the dangers of war; and to encourage independence movements."[51] With respect to the United States, Romania had its own objectives. In 1964 the Romanian government expressed its interest in again obtaining Most Favored Nation trade status. Romania also wanted American loans and industrial construction, including an atomic power plant.[52] In 1964 diplomatic missions between the United States and Romania were raised from the consular level to embassy status—a significant nod from Washington.

Romania satisfied U.S. expectations. On April 22, 1964, in the midst of the ideological conflict then raging between Moscow and Beijing, the Romanian Communist party plenum adopted a declaration that emphasized Romania's sovereignty and national independence. As Harrington and Courtney write, "On October 31, 1964, Romania unilaterally cut its armed forces from 240,000 men to 200,000 and reduced the length of conscription from 24 months to 18 months. . . . To further reduce Soviet influence in Romania, Gheorghiu-Dej refused to permit further Warsaw Pact military maneuvers on Romanian soil."[53] Between October and December of that year, Romanian authorities arranged for Soviet advisers of the Securitate to be removed from Romania.[54]

As Romania improved its relations with the United States, its ties with the USSR deteriorated. In seeking to develop its foreign trade with the West, Romanian Communist authorities needed above all bank loans, credits, and commercial contracts. Thus their banking and commercial ventures with the West became increasingly daring for a Communist country. Almost any means were justified in moving toward the ultimate goal: hard currency. Whatever the West valued was exported and sold, including, as we shall see, human beings. But when it came to human sales, Romanian authorities acted with restraint. Appearances had to be maintained. Cash would not be exchanged directly.

On July 11, 1956, the Securitate had been reorganized into eleven directorates and seven departments. The most important directorates were Foreign Intelligence, Domestic Intelligence, and Counterespionage.[55] The Foreign Intelligence directorate, which heavily infiltrated the ministries of foreign affairs and foreign trade, directly controlled Romania's trade in human beings.

According to General Ion Mihai Pacepa, First Secretary Gheorghiu-Dej alone did not have the courage to approve such a delicate matter. Khrushchev, on vacation in Romania in October 1958, persuaded him to do so.

Khrushchev insisted that the Foreign Intelligence directorate of the DGIE accept merchandise rather than money from the Israelis in return for Jewish emigrants, so that if news of the operation were leaked, the revelations would not damage Romania.[56]

Initially the DGIE pursued the trade in human beings through an intermediary. Henry Jacober, a Jewish businessman living in London, in the late fifties paid Romanian intelligence in cash given to him by private individuals in the West for exit visas for their relatives—free or imprisoned, Jewish or non-Jewish.[57] Born in 1900 in Munkacevo, and an escapee in 1938 to Great Britain from anti-Semitic Hungary, Jacober was described by Phyllis Yadin, his assistant from 1962, as a kind and compassionate businessman, one whose commercial dealings with Romania and Eastern Europe were prompted by philanthropic motives. Jewish families allowed to leave Romania under arrangements made by Jacober confirm this description. He received more than a hundred letters a week from families living in the West and in Israel who were willing to pay for the release of their relatives. Jacober handled transactions through two or three major Swiss banks.

The ransom, according to Dennis Deletant, varied between $4,000 and $6,000 for each. "The procedure was as follows: Jacober was approached at his address at 55 Park Lane in London and given the name of the person to be ransomed. He then gave the name a reference number, which was quoted in all correspondence, and took the details to Bucharest. There the ransom fee was fixed by the Romanian intelligence directorate acting on Dej's orders and communicated to Jacober, who on his return to Britain gave instructions to those paying the ransom to deposit the sum into Jacober's account at the Credit Suisse bank in Lucerne, Switzerland. The monies were only paid over to the Romanian authorities after the ransomed person had arrived in the West. In one such case a ransom of $4,200 was paid in August 1962 by relatives and friends for the release from prison of Maria Golescu, the librarian of the British Information Office in Bucharest."[58]

Another cash transaction involved pastor Richard Wurmbrand, a converted Jew and Lutheran minister imprisoned for many years in the Romanian gulag. In December 1964, according to the *Guardian*, the "Reverend Stuart Harris, head of the European Christian Mission, held a clandestine meeting with a tall, gaunt figure in a Bucharest park . . . who accepted a ransom of $10,000 . . . [a] financial temptation to which the Communist regime succumbed."[59]

By the late 1950s and early 1960s, both the Romanian authorities and Jacober preferred to handle emigration payments not in cash but in agricultural products. Jacober owned two companies in Great Britain: Jacober & Co. and Lineage Livestock Ltd. According to Yadin, after Jacober negotiated a fee with the Romanians—mostly with the head of the DGIE office in Great Britain, Colonel (later General) Gheorghe Marcu, who was stationed at the Romanian embassy in London under the cover of foreign trade—the funds were sent to an account in Switzerland and were used to purchase agricultural products. Jacober bought cattle from the Netherlands and sent the livestock to Romania in exchange for Jews and, though fewer in number, non-Jews.[60]

General Pacepa confirms Yadin's testimony: "Year after year DGIE became more deeply involved in Jewish emigration. It had not only to manage the 'the Jacober-Marcu gentleman's agreement' but also to obtain the best breeds of

animals and transport them to Romania on chartered air-
planes also paid for by Jacober. The diplomatic pouch was
carrying more bull sperm obtained with Jacober's help than
it was secret information."[61]

Israeli authorities quickly discovered Jacober's arrangements with the Romanians, and the Israeli Liaison Bureau
was irritated. Emigration was no place for private enterprise; it was and ought to remain a state matter. The bureau
asked Shaike Dan to solve the matter. Dan, in an interview
with Amos Ettinger, described Jacober: "That Jew had a
reputation of being willing to dip his hand into anything
that would fatten his bank account. I in the meantime had
learned other things about him. I knew that he was wealthy
and that as part of his business he helped a certain Eastern
European country [Romania] market its grain and corn in
Europe. . . . Coming and going between that country,
wheeling and dealing with the authorities there, he was
asked by wealthy people in West Europe to discuss the possibility of getting their relatives in the East out in return for
a fat payment. This involved only 'important' people, professors, physicians, whose relatives paid between five and
twenty thousand dollars per head. This Jew worked out
these deals in return for a handsome fee for the satisfaction
of all parties involved. Of course, this didn't involve hundreds of people, but dozens of Jews did get out this way."[62]
But Yadin says that Jacober did not receive a commission for
every person whose emigration he enabled, and that it was
not only "important people" but usually relatives in the
West who willingly paid the ransom.

In any event, in 1961 Dan asked a staff member of the
Israeli embassy in London to arrange a meeting with "that
Jewish emigré." "My objective," Dan recalls, "was to stop

his private business on the Jewish issue, which I saw as an opening for extortion on a grand scale. The meeting was scheduled for an early morning hour at the restaurant in the Dorchester Hotel in London. I didn't beat around the bush, and I hope that in my life I won't have to speak again to anyone in the language I used with him. I told him point-blank that he better withdraw from all business that involves payment for getting Jews out. If he did not stop it, I threatened [him with] the band that got Eichmann."[63] According to a high-ranking Israeli diplomat who chose to remain anonymous, Dan also warned Jacober, "The Thames is deep."

Dan continues, "The Jew, who at the beginning of the conversation still tried to keep up appearances, was now frightened and offered to continue to work only through me and only on missions I assigned him. Even though I didn't answer him on the spot, I knew I could now use his connections and services. In my head I already spun out plans for the emigration of thousands of more Jews. Before I put this man into operation, I went to talk to Shaul Avigur, who was then in London. It was with no light heart that I told Shaul about [Jacober], but I said to him that I see this man as another channel that may make large-scale immigration possible. No one could suspect Shaul of being less interested in *alyah* than Shaike Dan, but since the days of Alyah Beth Mossad, I knew that Shaul couldn't easily swallow the fact that we worked hand in hand with pirates and lowlifes. At those times I would always say to him: 'This work can't be done with chief rabbis, only with shady types like these.'"

Dan was persistent. "Shaul didn't let up, and asked that I arrange a meeting between him and [Jacober] so he could take his measure. Knowing Shaul as I did, I had reason to fear such a meeting, but I did what he wanted. We met in that Jew's home in one of the swankiest sections of London. Lots of art objects and Judaica were evidence of the fact that the man was from a religious background. In the conversation between us, the subject of the commission the man would receive for his services came up again. Shaul, who couldn't grasp that there was a word in the human vocabulary such as 'commission,' could see us making deals with *goyim*, with Turks or Greeks, but was shocked to hear that we'd have to pay a commission to a Jew as a fee for rescuing Jews. Shaul left the meeting more despairing than when he arrived. The next day he asked me to drop by his room at the Cumberland Hotel before he left London.

"I came about an hour before his flight. Without saying anything else he pronounced his decision: 'That won't work; that won't come out!' Plans to get more Jews out were already racing through my head, and I said to Shaul—I quote myself word for word: 'Every country has just one prime minister. This is going to be decided not by me and not by you but by Ben-Gurion.' And I added: 'The prime minister may decide as you see it, but on this I will accept judgment only after Ben-Gurion decides.' You have to know Shaul to realize how rare it was for someone to challenge his authority. It wasn't the first time I had argued with him, and not the first time a dispute between us was brought to a higher authority to be settled.

"To review the issue with Ben-Gurion, I also invited Golda Meir. I wanted her to be present, to hear her view too. To this day it's not clear to me why at that meeting she didn't open her mouth. Ben-Gurion listened patiently to Shaul, who spoke about extortion and heard me speak about another opening leading to the immigration of Jews to Israel. In the end he said: 'What Shaike is proposing is very grave. . . . But in Shaike's words I hear fervor, vision, and belief that it will succeed, and I authorize him to act to the best of his understanding.' Shaul was astounded by Ben-Gurion's reaction and simply did not believe his ears. Without telling me, he asked Ben-Gurion for written authorization. Only much later, Ben-Gurion's secretary, Hayim Yisraeli, told me that written authorization had been done. I had a lot of trouble with [Jacober], but the fact is that between 1961 and 1966 many Jews emigrated to Israel with his help."[64]

In February 1975, three months before his death, Jacober was still in business, albeit under Israeli supervision, and was receiving letters of gratitude from the families of released Romanian Jews. He was also instrumental in the release of about a thousand Jews from the Romanian penitentiary system.

After his meeting with Dan, an intimidated Jacober asked for an "emergency meeting" with Gheorghe Marcu. Jacober explained that he had made Israeli foreign intelligence aware of his contact with Romanian intelligence, and that Israel wished to use him for a top-secret operation. Israel was ready to pay the Romanian government an unstated sum for each Jew allowed to emigrate, based on a gentleman's agreement between Jacober and Marcu. Although Bucharest at first rejected the proposal, considering it a provocation, Jacober persisted. Several months later he proposed to build an automated chicken farm in Romania, free of charge, if five hundred Jewish families were allowed to leave. President Gheorghiu-Dej approved the proposal as a one-time experiment, and before the end of the year a modern chicken farm was installed in Periş. When Gheorghiu-Dej visited, he liked it so much that he approved five hundred exit visas and ordered five more chicken farms.[65]

What began as an experiment with Jacober soon became a major operation. The cash-starved Romanian economy found these trade-generated farms a great boost to its exports. General Pacepa, the highest-ranking defector in Communist history, describes this remarkable story: "By the end of 1964, the Ministry of the Interior had become the largest meat producer in Romania. It owned chicken farms, turkey farms, and pig farms producing tens of thousands of animals a year, several cattle farms, and other farms with some 100,000 head of sheep—all with automated slaughterhouses, refrigerated storehouses, and packing plants. To transport the packaged meat it also had a TIR [European International Road] fleet of refrigerated Mercedes trucks. In early 1965 a Kellogg's Corn Flakes factory was added to the ministry's food line."[66]

Pacepa describes how these farms and food processing plants—built in Periş and operated by political prisoners—were paid for by Henry Jacober in exchange for exit visas for Romanian Jews. When the labor force was lean, Pacepa writes, Gheorghiu-Dej would simply say to Alexandru Draghici, the minister of the interior, "If you cannot find the people you need in the jails, just arrest the ones you need and then use them." Deputy Minister of the Interior Alexandru Danescu was placed in charge of the farms, and output was exported only to the West. Henry Jacober helped these exports both directly and indirectly. By the mid-1960s the annual authorization of emigration visas for Romanian Jews was, according to Pacepa, "entirely dependent upon eggs, chicken, turkey, pork, beef, and corn flakes exported to the West."[67]

Pacepa reports that live Danish Landrace pigs, "anesthetized and transported first in diplomatic automobiles, then in special diplomatic pouches, and finally in large TIR trucks protected in special diplomatic seals," were smuggled out of Denmark with Jacober's help. By 1965, Romania annually produced fifty thousand Landrace pigs, "all exported to the West as bacon and ham with Jacober's help."[68]

The money obtained from these agricultural exports (between $8 million and $10 million a year) was kept in a secret account to which only Gheorghiu-Dej had access. Prime Minister Maurer was kept in the dark about the exchange, and only six officers in the DGIE knew of Israel's role in the creation of Romania's new farms.[69]

5

An Uneasy Relationship

As Romania sought independence from the Soviet bloc, relations with Moscow grew increasingly acrimonious. Romania's refusal to side with the Soviet Union in the Sino-Soviet conflict was a major point of contention. And when Bucharest suggested that it no longer wished to have Soviet secret police advisers in the country, the head of the Soviet KGB, Vladimir Semichastny, and its director of foreign intelligence, Alexander Sakharovsky, were furious. They visited Bucharest in an effort to persuade the Romanians to change their minds, but their visits were to no avail.[1]

Nicolae Ceausescu, who came to power in 1965, had become suspicious of the KGB owing to its alleged involvement in Gheorghiu-Dej's death (Dej had died of lung cancer—the rumor in Bucharest was that he had been irradiated by the KGB).[2] Consequently Ceausescu closely supervised cooperation between the Securitate and Soviet and East European intelligence agencies, prohibited the East German Stasi from establishing a liaison office in Bucharest, and thwarted Soviet efforts to involve the Romanian secret police in a smear campaign against the Vatican and its supporters.[3]

As Romania shifted its diplomatic and trade relations from the Soviet Union to the West, its policy toward Israel also changed. Yosef Govrin, Israeli ambassador to Romania between 1985 and 1989, recalled that Ceausescu played his "Jewish and Israel card in order to advance Romania's interests in the West."[4] Dennis Deletant writes that "Ceausescu's policies toward the Jews can be summed up in a few words: to let those who so wished emigrate in order to facilitate the process of creating a homogeneous Romania based on the majority Romanian element."[5] Ambassador Govrin elaborates: "At least two motives prompted Romania to permit *alyah* to Israel: first, to solve in this manner the Jewish question in Romania, gradually ridding itself of the Jews, thus vacating their jobs for Romanian workers, *besides receiving payment from Israel for each emigrant depending on their age and education*; second, demonstrating consideration of demands by Israel and the West to let the Jews leave Romania as a humanitarian act. . . ."[6] Liviu Turcu, former chief of the North American and Western European departments of the CIE (successor to the DGIE and DIE) and one of the most important CIE defectors, later observed that Ceausescu looked upon the rapidly diminishing Jewish community in Romania as hostages; their general exodus would deprive him of a crucial bargaining chip with Israel and the United States.[7] He would dole them out gradually.

From 1958, when Romania again opened its doors, until 1965, when Dej died, 107,540 Romanian Jews emigrated to Israel. On average, 13,487 Jews emigrated annually; the numbers peaked in 1961 when 21,269 Jews emigrated, and in 1964 when 25,926 left. In 1965, with the advent of

Ceausescu, 10,949 Jews emigrated to Israel; by 1966, the numbers had dropped to 3,647. The years 1967 and 1968 were disastrous, with 779 and 226 Jews respectively allowed to emigrate. Between 1969 and Ceausescu's fall from power in 1989, Jewish emigration to Israel stabilized at an annual average rate of 1,997.

The 1967 Six-Day War between Israel and the Arab nations was partly to blame for the dramatic decline in emigration in 1966 and 1968. Romanian authorities had no wish to antagonize the defeated Arab states, which condemned Jewish emigration to Israel. Yet, as Pacepa notes, there were also personal reasons. The "Jacober-Marcu gentleman's agreement was kept in deepest secrecy. Prime Minister Ion Gheorghe Maurer, who was also Gheorghiu-Dej's best personal friend, did not know a thing about it. Ceausescu himself learned of this operation only in 1965, when he came to power. He denounced the setup as 'outrageous,' transferred the farms to the Ministry of Agriculture, fired Marcu from DGIE, and drastically reduced Jewish emigration."[8]

Pacepa reveals that Ceausescu was informed of the DGIE's sale of Jews during a private encounter with the head of the directorate, General Nicolae Doicaru. Immediately after Ceausescu met with DGIE management, Pacepa recalls, "I was waiting in the anteroom of Ceausescu's office, and I could hear him screaming hysterically. From Doicaru I later learned that his revelation about the 'Jacober affair' generated a kind of 'nuclear explosion.' Ceausescu's first reaction was to accuse the former minister of the interior, Alexandru Draghici (who had coordinated the 'Jacober affair' during Gheorghiu-Dej's reign), of being an 'enemy of the Communist party' for wanting to destroy Romania's international prestige.[9]

"Two years later," Pacepa continues, "Ceausescu had second thoughts . . . and asked if Jacober was still alive. Soon after, Marcu was reinstated in the DGIE, promoted in rank and position, and ordered secretly to resume contact with Jacober. . . . This operation now became more secret than ever."[10]

Under Shaike Dan's supervision, Jacober resumed his role in the emigration of Romanian Jews to Israel. But Jacober's importance waned under the close supervision of Dan, whose role in negotiations increased. Ceausescu was now pleased to have a direct connection with the Israeli government, but he ordered that it be maintained simply as a personal relationship between Dan and Marcu and kept secret.[11] According to a former Israeli diplomat, Golda Meir literally told the Romanian authorities, "Let [the Jews] go, and we will help you."[12]

Now that he was directly involved in the sale of Jews to Israel, Ceausescu ordered the DGIE to shift gears from the "ancient age of barter" to "modern foreign trade." He wanted "cold dollars." He also ordered the DGIE to contact the Mossad directly in order to eliminate the commission that Tel Aviv paid Jacober for his role as mediator.[13] Ceausescu directed that the new gentleman's agreement provide that "Bucharest would be paid in cash a certain amount per head, depending on age, education, profession, employment, and family status, for each Jew allowed to emigrate."[14] Marcu and Dan met monthly at Romanian embassies in West Germany, Austria, and Switzerland. Marcu brought lists containing the names of Jews approved for emigration; Dan brought suitcases of American dollars.[15] One of Dan's associates, Yanai Motke, would also travel to Romania with a diplomatic suitcase that usually contained half a million dollars. On the occasion of one delivery to a member of the secret police, the man looked at the suitcase and complained, "Next time bring Samsonite."[16]

Eventually Ceausescu himself met with Dan. Cornel Burtica, former minister of foreign trade and later member of the Politburo of the Romanian Communist party, recalls: "During the summer of 1969 . . . Ceausescu, who was hunting somewhere in Lapusna, called me on the phone and told me: 'There is an envoy of the Israeli government, one Dan, who is due to arrive. Receive him, talk to him, but don't start any negotiations until I get back.'"[17] Burtica continues, "This is how I met Dan. . . . We discussed the numbers [of would-be Jewish emigrants], and he asked me if the numbers of emigrants could be augmented. Ceausescu told me that he had discussed this with [Dan] and that they had agreed on numbers and means of payment, the technical part being left to discussion by the Securitate and the Finance [Ministry]. . . . All major decisions, including this one, were made by Ceausescu."[18]

Ceausescu maintained strict secrecy about the negotiations and exchange. He removed the DGIE's name from the new agreement and spread a disinformation story that Marcu had been withdrawn from the DGIE and appointed deputy director general of the Institute of World Economy, a cover-up institution staffed by DGIE officers.[19] Burtica confirms that the Institute had a few dozen genuine researchers and a few hundred foreign intelligence officers.[20] It was a military unit within the DGIE; hundreds of DGIE officers received Institute identification without ever entering its doors. Only Marcu kept an office there.[21]

On November 10, 1969, the Dan-Marcu gentleman's agreement became an unsigned but written protocol that would be valid for three years. It stated that Romania agreed to allow 40,000 Jews to emigrate to Israel: 2,000 in 1969, 12,800 in 1970, 16,000 in 1971, and 9,200 between January and October 1972. The protocol also noted that of the 40,000 emigrants, Romanian authorities would permit 10 percent to have university degrees, another 10 percent to be qualified workers and technicians allowed to take their diplomas with them, and 2 percent to be students. The protocol mentioned no price tags, only that Tarom, the Romanian national airline, would provide transportation.[22] According to a former Israeli diplomat, transport negotiations were particularly thorny. When the Romanians demanded full-fare prices, the Israelis were outraged. Ultimately the negotiators settled for charter-priced airline tickets paid for by the Israelis.

The Romanian government did not entirely honor its side of the protocol. Although it specified that 2,000 Jews could emigrate to Israel between November 10 and December 31, 1969, only 1,754 Jews were actually released; and though the protocol stated that between 1970 and 1972 an additional 38,000 Jews would be released, in fact a mere 10,480 were allowed to emigrate.

When Israel's Ministry of Foreign Affairs asked Valeriu Georgescu, the first Romanian ambassador to Israel, to explain the reduced figures, he replied that "certain paragraphs of the previous agreement, especially those concerning the prohibiting of publicity on this subject, were not respected by the Israeli side."[23] Despite this conflict, the protocol substantially increased the number of Jews allowed to emigrate to Israel.

After 1972, agreements of this type were signed by the Romanian and Israeli representatives every five years.

Probably sometime in late 1972 or early 1973, and certainly again in 1978, similar secret protocols were signed.

When Dan traveled to Bucharest for this business, he normally met with his counterpart, General Marcu. A 1964 photograph shows him in front of Ateneul Roman, the city's main concert hall, smiling and smoking a cigar. On one visit he met with Marcu and Pacepa's boss, General Doicaru, head of the DGIE. Difficult to impress, Dan confessed to one of his Liaison Bureau colleagues in Tel Aviv: "I met a hangman."

In his efforts to negotiate the emigration of Romanian Jews to Israel, Dan was also forced to ask Israeli authorities to release Romanian spies held in Israeli prisons. In January 1965 the former Securitate Colonel Francisc (Efraim) Samuel, who had emigrated to Israel in 1958, was arrested for espionage on behalf of the Romanians. He had used a radio and drop boxes to report to Bucharest. His handler, a Romanian diplomat, was expelled, and Samuel was condemned by a court in Haifa to six years in prison.

Romania pressured Israel to free the colonel. President Ceausescu became personally involved in the case and even threatened to stop the emigration of Jews to Israel if Samuel were not immediately released and returned to Romania.[24] According to the Israeli journalist Tesu Solomovici, Dan, fearing that Ceausescu would make good on his threat, spoke directly to Prime Minister Levi Eshkol; Samuel was immediately released.[25] DIE attempts to recruit Romanian Jews as spies in Israel did not end with this episode. According to a 1978 Securitate internal investigation, during 1969–1970 about 250 Romanian Jews who had made *alyah* reported to Israeli authorities that they had been recruited in Romania for espionage activities in Israel.[26]

Dan's involvement in the emigration of Romanian Jews apparently made him a prime political target of Soviet and Arab agents. According to the historians Raviv and Melman, Charles Jordan—an American citizen and senior official for the Joint—disappeared after arriving in Prague on August 14, 1967. "It can now be stated with near certainty that Charles Jordan was murdered—in a case of mistaken identity—by Communist agents. They believed that their victim was Shaike Dan."[27]

Before visiting Prague, Jordan had gone to Bucharest. In his memoirs, Rosen describes an attempt by a couple in a car with Belgian license plates to kidnap and poison him. If these events did in fact occur, it is unlikely that the DGIE was behind them, for its members had no interest in eliminating Dan or Jordan. That said, according to Rosen, Jordan was kidnapped in Prague by the Egyptian secret service, taken to the United Arab Republic embassy, killed in a struggle during his interrogation, and his body dumped in the Vltava River. Rosen claims that members of Czechoslovakia's secret service witnessed Jordan's kidnapping and the disposal of his body, and had orders not to interfere.[28] In an interview with Amos Ettinger, Dan acknowledged that it was possible his identity was mistaken, but added: "If I really was targeted for murder, in this instance it is not really clear [that they intended to kill me]."[29]

When Ceausescu came to power in 1965, he reorganized the Securitate and its Foreign Intelligence branch several times, first in 1967, and again in 1972 and 1973. He aimed to modernize the Romanian secret service and increase its power without diminishing its repressive role or interfering with its reporting directly to him. In 1972 he changed the service's name from the DGIE to DIE.[30] (In 1978, after Pacepa's defection, it would become the CIE.) The DIE became an important espionage as well as economic force for Romania, as Ceausescu dramatically increased its power to obtain hard currency by any means.[31]

As Ceausescu was reorganizing the Securitate, Tel Aviv's Liaison Bureau was undergoing a major leadership change. In March 1970, Nehemiah Levanon replaced Shaul Avigur at the Liaison Bureau, thus filling the "oversized shoes," as Raviv and Melman write, "of one of the founding grandfathers of Israeli intelligence." Avigur had retired in his seventies in poor health after seventeen years of commanding the bureau's secret fight for Soviet Jewry. Levanon had worked for Avigur at the bureau and earlier in the institute for Alyah Beth. "Posted to Moscow as a diplomat in the 1950s," Raviv and Melman write, "Levanon was expelled by the Soviets for [having] clandestine contacts with the Jews. . . . Levanon returned to Israel and worked at the Liaison Bureau headquarters in Tel Aviv and was then posted at the Israeli embassy in Washington to take charge of Jewish affairs—mainly lobbying among American politicians and officials on behalf of emigration from the Soviet Union."[32]

Dan, maintaining his pivotal role as a contact between Israel and the Romanian leadership, was briefly the chief of Vienna's Liaison Bureau. In this capacity he ensured that Romanian Jewish emigrés flew directly from Bucharest to Tel Aviv rather than stopping over in Austria, Italy, or France. He thereby increased the number of Jews who made it to Israel, and circumvented the Securitate, which used the CIE debriefing of Romanian emigrés in Austria and Italy as a pretext to slow and even cancel the issuance of visas.[33]

By the early 1970s, Ceausescu had completed what his predecessor had only begun: he had quietly, systematically, efficiently, and almost entirely purged almost every Jew from positions of importance in Romania. To deflect international suspicion, Ceausescu kept a handful of Jews—especially those he liked—in visible positions. Ambassador Govrin observes that those remaining were "born Jewish but attempted with all their might to assimilate into Romanian society and culture. And the more they tried, the less inclined were Romanian nationalists in the local hierarchy to absorb them. Therefore we find that not a single Jew at this time served in the higher echelons of the ministries of defense or foreign affairs; nor, if I am not mistaken, in any other ministries."[34] According to Deletant, however, the remaining Jews possessed newfound freedoms. Under Ceausescu, "the status enjoyed by the Jewish community was unique in the whole Communist bloc. The Jews enjoyed what one scholar described as 'possibly the greatest measure of autonomy among all denominations.' This he attributed to their contracting numbers leaving a predominantly elderly community, which posed no threat to the regime or to Ceausescu's desire to promote a favorable image in the West. . . ."[35] Rabbi Rosen serves Ambassador Govrin as a useful example of Jewish freedom in Ceausescu's Romania: He "was the only rabbi in the whole Communist sphere who gave . . . sermons publicly, and he used to recite a prayer every Saturday and on Jewish festivals for the well-being of the state of Israel, its ministers, its advisers. This was a courageous act that was not even performed by all rabbis in the West."[36]

A controversial figure within and beyond Romania's borders, Rosen, according to Govrin, aroused resentment in certain Jewish circles in Romania as well as among some of Israel's envoys in Bucharest: "Perhaps [it was] due to the forceful way he ruled the community, even to the manifestation of totalitarian trappings in his immediate surroundings, or maybe owing to suspicions of his collaborating with the Communist regime, since on his visits to the West he customarily praised the authorities' attitude to the Jewish minority during the Ceausescu period. . . ."[37] Rosen was also suspected of collaboration with the Communist authorities for his help in trying to obtain Most Favored Nation trade status for Romania.

Although human rights were neglected in Romania as in other Communist countries, Rosen played a seminal role in the emigration of Romanian Jews to Israel. But he could not have done so without the help he received from Israel, the United States, and Jewish organizations in the West. He was also a force of change within Romania: he fought for the national rights of the Jewish minority promised by the constitution—such as the right for religious education—and publicly demanded the eradication of anti-Semitism.

In lockstep with the Romanian Communist party tradition of the 1950s, Ceausescu and his agents kept the Jewish community's activities under tight surveillance. Indeed, from 1948 to the fall of the Communist regime in 1989, all of Rosen's movements and those of the Jewish community were monitored and recorded by dozens of secret police officers. Hundreds of community informants assisted; neighbors reported on each other; and U.S. and Israeli contacts were followed, their conversations secretly transcribed or taped.

In April 1967, for example, Nahum Goldman, chairman of the World Jewish Congress, visited Bucharest with Gerhard Riegner. For reasons unknown, the Jewish community's technician could not record Goldman's speech at the Athenee Palace Hotel. Both Rosen and Goldman wished to have the speech recorded in order to have Goldman on tape saying, "It is possible for Jews to live a full life under Communist rule." Two or three months later, Rosen related the story to Bodnaras. Smiling, Bodnaras responded to Rosen: "Tell Goldman not to worry; we have a tape of the entire speech."[38]

Microphones were installed in Rosen's office (as well as in synagogues, Jewish schools, and hospitals). In order to control his activities, Securitate officers often tried to intimidate him. While officers of the internal Securitate bugged Rosen's private residence and organized a network of informants around him, DIE agents discreetly visited him at his office at the Federation of Jewish Communities, especially when Rosen returned from his frequent travels abroad.[39] DIE (later CIE) leaders maintained a close relationship with Rosen, whose code name as a CIE informant in the late 1980s was GX 21.[40] Before 1977, Rosen's main DIE contacts were General Romeo Popescu and Colonels Dumitru Popescu, Ion Pasca, and Nicolae Spataru; after 1978 his main CIE contact was General Alexandru "Bebe" Tanasescu (alias Florin Margarit).[41]

The years 1967 and 1968 were outstanding in the history of Romanian diplomacy. In January 1967, Romania was, to the chagrin of East Germany (the German Democratic Republic, or GDR), the first Eastern European Communist country to establish diplomatic relations with West Germany. A U.S. report noted: "Despite Ceausescu's opposition to emigration, [Romania's] ethnic German population declined sharply. In 1967, when diplomatic relations with

West Germany were established, roughly 60,000 ethnic Germans requested permission to emigrate. By 1978, some 80,000 had departed for West Germany."[42]

Romania sold not only its Jews. Encouraged by results in the Jewish trade, Ceausescu ordered the DIE to initiate a similar operation for ethnic Germans, which he considered potentially even more lucrative. Pacepa writes, "There were at that time more ethnic Germans than Jews left in Romania. The sale of ethnic Germans was arranged along the same lines, based on a personal agreement between the same Marcu and 'Eduard,' who represented himself as an undercover intelligence officer and personal representative of Hans-Dietrich Genscher, the West German minister of the interior, who was directly involved with facilitating the emigration of Germans from Eastern Europe. . . . Suitcases full of U.S. dollars were transported monthly to Bucharest via the Romanian airline Tarom, and special credits with part of the interest paid by 'Eduard' were periodically issued to maintain or stimulate Ceausescu's enthusiasm for the emigration of *Volksdeutsche* to the fatherland."[43]

Eduard, according to Pacepa, was in fact Edgar Hirt, a negotiator for West Germany not only with Romania but also with the German Democratic Republic, a country equally involved in the general trade of dissidents, family reunification, and spy swapping.[44] Hirt had one order from Egon Franke, the minister of inter-German relations: "Keep it quiet." Hirt negotiated deals with Wolfgang Vogel, an East German lawyer with strong Stasi connections.[45]

When in June 1967 Israeli forces swiftly and mercilessly crushed the Egyptian, Jordanian, and Syrian armies, the so-called Six-Day War was a major defeat not only for the Arab world but also for the Soviet Union and its satellites, which for years had economically and ideologically supported Egypt and Syria. As the Israeli historian Howard Sachar writes, "On June 9, the Communist bloc leaders gathered in Moscow, where seven of them issued a long declaration of solidarity with the Arab cause, promising help to the Arab nations should Israel continue its 'aggression.' Within the next few days all Communist governments except Romania severed diplomatic relations with Israel."[46] Romania refused to sign the Moscow Declaration. By June 1967, through a declaration issued as Document 7972 of the UN Security Council, Romania had positioned itself as a potential mediator between Israel and its adversaries.[47]

From December 1966, Israel had supported the election of Romania's foreign minister, Corneliu Manescu, as chairman of the UN General Assembly.[48] Bucharest was not unmindful. With respect to the Arab-Israeli conflict, Romania's position was that Israel should withdraw from the occupied territories and have its security provided by an international guarantee and honored by its neighbors. In an interview with the Dutch paper *Haagse Post* on July 29, 1967, Prime Minister Ion Gheorghe Maurer declared: "Like the Dutch leaders, we feel that no state should be threatened with destruction just because it was created in a somewhat exceptional manner. . . . That state has been founded and the people have installed themselves in the country, and it won't do to say: Let us cut the throats of three million people. That does not provide any solution to the problem. . . . We are of the opinion that there is a certain amount of logic in the viewpoint that the Israeli troops cannot be withdrawn without guarantees. Ten years ago the Israelis faced the same situation. They were told to withdraw, and they did so. Ten years afterward the same condition is being raised, and at the present time I feel that the Israelis should at least receive some kind of guarantee to ensure that the same thing does not happen again in ten years' time."[49]

In August 1968, Ceausescu strongly opposed Soviet intervention in Czechoslovakia, fearful of the threat to his own regime. He accelerated Romania's pro-Western foreign policy, which both fellow citizens and Western chancelleries admired. Yet the Romanian Communist party's domestic policies remained Stalinist and nationalistic. Diplomatic relations with Israel thus served a useful purpose: they enabled Romania to emphasize its difference from the Soviet Union and the rest of the East European Communist bloc. In September 1968, during a discussion in Bucharest, Ceausescu declared that the withdrawal of Israeli troops from the occupied territories "must be coupled with the recognition by the Arabs of Israel's right to exist." When a British official at the meeting replied that the Israelis should be asked to withdraw only under conditions that guaranteed their security, Bodnaras agreed.[50]

Israeli-Romanian economic relations continued to develop and were now broadened to include armaments. The Romanians were most interested in tanks. In January 1969, Romanian authorities denied rumors that Israel had proposed to sell Romania Soviet tanks captured during the Six-Day War at a reduced price.[51]

Yet this was not a baseless rumor. According to Raviv and Melman, the Israeli military and Romania had a history of working together: "Israeli experts serviced Romanian tanks and other military equipment" in return for "Ceausescu's agreement to permit the departure of Romania's Jewish citizens."[52] In the 1970s, Pacepa recalls, Shaike Dan delivered a Centurion tank to the DIE "at Marcu's request, and in return Marcu promised him that such a gesture would be followed by an increase in Jewish emigration from Romania." Ceausescu was ecstatic and asked Marcu to obtain the blueprint for the tank as well.[53] According to a former Israeli diplomat, Romania also asked Dan for up-to-date computers. When the equipment offered by Israel did not satisfy the Romanians, the deal fell through. Dan, commenting on his complicated relationship with the Romanian authorities, says: "My relations with the Romanians became so close, they even allowed themselves to ask unpopular things from me. If I was able to help them, I did so willingly. I'll say no more than that many of their requests had to do with weighty matters."[54] In June 1982, the Israeli defense minister Ariel Sharon made a secret visit to Romania—arranged by Mossad—and offered, according to Melman and Raviv, "technological cooperation." He was joined by experts from the Israeli military and aircraft industries.[55]

Armaments were not the only topic of conversation between the two countries. Romania and Israel also negotiated problems related to raising their diplomatic representation to embassy level. Fearing an Arab reaction, Romania postponed an official agreement for months and preferred to negotiate it behind closed doors. Romania's delay made the Israelis anxious. Abba Eban, Israel's foreign minister, told Bucharest that the Arab world should not be allowed to dictate Israeli-Romanian relations.[56]

On August 17, 1969, Romania agreed to elevate relations with Israel to the ambassadorial level. Meanwhile Romania continued to support "the struggle of the Arab people to defend their national independence and sovereignty" and called for a negotiated settlement of the Middle East conflict.[57]

Earlier that month, in a major diplomatic victory for Bucharest and to the delight of Ceausescu, President Nixon visited Romania. As Harrington and Courtney write, "Ceausescu welcomed Nixon . . . complete with honor guard and a twenty-one-gun salute." Nixon wanted Ceausescu to act as a mediator between Washington and Beijing, and to help in the resolution of the Vietnam conflict. Ceausescu agreed. In return, he wanted Most Favored Nation trade status for Romania.[58]

Romania's entreaties to the West annoyed the Kremlin. Although the two countries maintained economic relations, Romania and the USSR mistrusted each other. After Nixon's visit to Romania, the KGB began sending its "illegals," disguised as Western journalists, to Bucharest. As the Russian defector Vasili Mitrokhin writes, "The KGB reports on Romania were written in a tone that combined indignation with deep suspicion. . . . The illegals sent to Romania under Western disguise in 1971 were ordered to collect intelligence on Romanian relations with the United States and China; Romanian claims on Soviet territory in Bessarabia and north Bukovina; the political and economic basis of opposition to the Soviet Union. . . . The priority given to Romania reflected growing Soviet displeasure at the foreign policy of its leader, Nicolae Ceausescu."[59]

Ceausescu needed the United States in his struggle for independence from the Soviet Union; he viewed Israel as the key that would unlock the American vault of support. When Israel's foreign minister Moshe Dayan visited Bucharest in April 1978, Ceausescu asked him to put in a good word with Washington for Most Favored Nation status for Romania. Dayan replied, "I will talk to our ambassador in Washington, and I promise you, Mr. President, that we will do everything we can."[60]

Dayan's visit to Bucharest involved continuing negotiations on Jewish emigration to Israel. Dan arranged for the foreign minister's political adviser, Eli Rubinstein, to brief Dayan thoroughly, and insisted that "under no circumstances should [Dayan] mention the word immigration. The expression 'family reunification' was and still is the formula accepted by us and by them in Romania."[61]

The rise to embassy-level diplomatic relations between Israel and Romania coincided with increased Arab-sponsored terrorism against Israeli targets in Europe and the persecution of Jews in Arab countries. On January 27, 1969, as Howard M. Sachar notes, "Nine Jews among fourteen prisoners [were] hanged as 'spies' in Baghdad's Liberation Square; crowds estimated at 200,000 marched past the dangling corpses as the onlookers were treated to a running loudspeaker commentary on Jewish 'treason.' Libyan Jewry shared in this intensified persecution. Following the June War, hundreds of Jewish shops were burned again, as in 1945 . . . two-thirds of the remaining 4,000 Jews fled to Europe, the rest to Israel."[62]

Israel was irritated by Romania's political ambiguity: either it spoke indifferently about Arab terrorist acts against Israel or ignored them altogether. A month after the incident in Iraq, Eliezer Doron, head of the Israeli legation in Bucharest, confronted Corneliu Manescu, the Romanian foreign minister, on this issue. Doron brought up the recent terrorist attack against an Israeli plane at the Zurich airport, and expressed his frustration that Romania's government-controlled newspapers had ignored it—yet had condemned Israeli action in Beirut.[63] Manescu lamely equivocated.

Romania steered a treacherous course in attempting to balance its political allegiances between the Arab states and Israel. High-ranking Romanian officials, including Ceausescu, continued to meet with their Arab counterparts, stressing their "brotherly" relations. Hafez al-Assad, Saddam Hussein, and Yasser Arafat were "comrades" to Ceausescu. At the same time Romania ordered its diplomats in Arab countries to keep their distance whenever the host government took actions that Israel might see as aggressive.

Egypt recalled its ambassador from Bucharest when Romania and Israel raised their diplomatic representation to embassy level. His replacement, the chargé d'affaires, blamed the recall on the "Jewish blood" of Prime Minister Maurer (whose origins in fact were German) and other Romanian Communist leaders.[64] In a diplomatic cable from Egypt, the Algerian ambassador to Baghdad, Ahmed Tanefile al-Madani, was reported to have declared in Baghdad that "the Arab countries that met to discuss the boycott against Israel decided to not boycott Romania because it was a 'socialist country,' but recommended reducing relations with Romania as long as this country continues to develop relations with Israel."[65] Egyptian foreign trade enterprises sought to impose specific anti-Israeli provisions on their Romanian counterparts in an effort to force Romania to boycott the Jewish state.[66]

Ceausescu, too, appeared sometimes irritated with Israel. In a meeting with Nahum Goldman, president of the World Jewish Congress held in May 1970 in Bucharest, Ceausescu spoke bitterly about Israel's current policies, calling its leaders "arrogant and silly." Romania had refused to end its relations with Israel "despite very great pressures." For Israel to insist on direct talks with the Arab countries,

Ceausescu claimed, was "nonsense and is an excuse for covering Israel's purpose not to withdraw from the occupied territories."[67]

In February 1970, owing to Israel's "military actions against the Arab countries and its repression of Palestine's liberation movement," the Politburo of the Romanian Communist party decided to "reduce and restrain cultural and diplomatic relations with Israel, [and] to condemn more firmly Israeli repression against the Arab countries." Yet simultaneously it would "develop economic relations with Israel, ensuring not to export strategic goods."[68] The party obviously did not regard Jews as a strategic good.

Arab leaders thought otherwise. In April 1971, Ceausescu met in Moscow with Abdel Moshen Aboul Nour, general secretary of Egypt's Arab Socialist Union. The historians Ionel Calafeteanu and Alexandru Cornescu-Coren write, "Nour stated that 'because the Jewish immigrants increase Israel's combat capacity,' [Egypt] wishes that 'this emigration be suspended until the end of the conflict.' Ceausescu tried to diminish the importance of the emigration, and stated that in 1970 'only 300 people' of Jewish origin left the country, but even those had 'other destinations, although it is possible that they changed their direction.' Furthermore, Ceausescu said that 'Romania took into account Nasser's opinion to restrain and maintain restrained Jewish emigration' but emphasized that 'total restrictions cannot be accepted.'"[69] Ceausescu lied to Nour: in 1970, 5,614 Romanian Jews had emigrated to Israel, a peak year under his rule.

Over the next several years a number of episodes indicated Romania's growing ties to Israel:

In the early 1970s, Romania cautiously attempted to mediate between the Arab countries at war with Israel. In

January 1971, on Israel's behalf, Romania asked Egypt about the fate of four wounded Israeli prisoners of war. The Romanian Ministry of Foreign Affairs instructed its ambassador in Cairo to leave no paper trail concerning this démarche.[70]

Between 1972 and 1973, the 1969 Jewish emigration protocol having expired, Dan and Marcu prepared a new one. Although he was not an official member of the Israeli delegation to Bucharest, Dan organized visits to Romania by Israeli prime ministers. These visits, he recalls, "became a feature of the political process. They were part of a way to get our word to the other countries of Eastern Europe and to the Arab states. . . . Ceausescu earned himself a reputation as a mediator. His attempts to be a peacemaker for the Middle East boosted his stock in the West, too. . . ."[71]

Dan continues, "Before Golda Meir left to visit Romania, I acted as intermediary in preparing the meeting between her and Ceausescu. . . . I said: 'When you discuss political matters, do that alone.'"[72] Jewish emigration and the peace process in the Middle East held Meir and Ceausescu in a fourteen-hour discussion; together they tried to arrange a meeting between Egyptian president Anwar Sadat and Prime Minister Golda Meir, but these efforts failed.

Dan was in Bucharest on Friday, May 5, 1972, when Pacepa, then deputy head of the DIE, received information from Beirut that four Arabs had left Cairo for Bucharest to assassinate Meir as she walked to the Chorale Temple. "At approximately five-thirty," Pacepa writes, "four Arabs, surprised and overwhelmed, were arrested on a street close to the synagogue without being able to use their submachine guns and grenades. All of them were carrying Egyptian passports."[73]

Ceausescu was furious and ordered the assassins killed. He soon changed his mind. The terrorists—photographed, fingerprinted, and lavishly fed—were expelled the following day. A few months later, with photographic evidence in hand, the DIE identified the leader of the terrorist team in the Meir operation as Abu Daud, the same person who planned the 1972 terrorist attack on the Israeli Olympic team in Munich.[74]

Her life spared by the DIE, Meir entered the Chorale Temple. Thousands of Jews crowded the temple, the courtyard, and neighboring streets. As Rosen writes, "More than one hundred boys and girls welcomed her, singing 'Shalom aleichem.' Golda was astonished . . . she began to cry. Her picture with the caption 'Golda Wipes Her Tears in Bucharest' appeared in all the Jewish newspapers."[75] But the Israeli-Romanian talks did not go well. At one point Meir even walked out of her discussions with Nicolae Ceausescu. The atmosphere improved only during the state dinner.

On November 10, 1975—the thirty-seventh anniversary of *Kristallnacht* in Nazi Germany—the UN General Assembly adopted a resolution equating Zionism with racism. In view of the entire assembly, Israel's UN ambassador, Chaim Herzog, tore up the UN resolution, and said, "Hitler would have felt himself at home were he present here today."[76] Unlike the Soviet Union and the Eastern European Communist bloc as well as the Arab countries, Romania maintained an ambiguous political voice and refused to vote on the resolution.

In 1977, Bucharest asked Shaike Dan if Menachem Begin, who had just been elected prime minister, would accept an invitation from Ceausescu to visit Romania. Dan recalls, "I had to tell Begin that behind this invitation was the president's sincere desire to serve as a mediator between us and Egypt."[77] Dan's appeal prevailed, and Ceausescu became the first head of state to meet with Prime Minister Begin.

Thoroughly briefed by Dan, Begin arrived in Bucharest on August 25, 1977. Ceausescu made known his desire to help broker a Middle East settlement. According to Sachar, "It was accordingly Ceausescu who arranged a secret parallel meeting in Bucharest between Begin and Said Merei, a representative of the Egyptian national assembly. To Merei as to Ceausescu, Begin emphasized his willingness to offer 'extensive satisfaction' on the Sinai, even to negotiate some form of self-governing Arab entity for Gaza and the West Bank. Merei in turn promised to convey Begin's message to Sadat."[78]

The Romanian authorities took extraordinary security measures during Begin's visit. Rosen describes one of them: "My wife and I . . . saw [Begin] disappear in the direction of the temple. Suddenly from another direction we saw another Begin coming toward us. This 'Begin' wore the same kind of clothes as the first one. His appearance was very similar, too. His entourage consisted of the same number of people, and he was accompanied by the same number of security men. Later I understood that two Begins had left the hotel, each taking a different route. The Romanian police feared an assassination attempt and wanted to confuse the plotters. I don't know whether they succeeded in confusing them; they certainly confused me."[79]

Abba Gefen, the Israeli ambassador to Bucharest, described the dramatic consequences of Begin's visit: "Ceausescu became convinced that the new prime minister of Israel sincerely wanted peace, and he invited President Sadat to come to Bucharest. Sadat arrived in October and asked . . . Ceausescu whether he was really convinced that Begin wanted peace and was able to sign it. Ceausescu answered both questions affirmatively."[80] In September 1977, Israeli foreign minister Dayan instructed Meir Rosenne, the foreign ministry's legal adviser, to draft an Egyptian-Israeli peace treaty.[81]

Twelve months later Begin and Sadat signed the Camp David agreements. Ceausescu was shocked that he did not receive the Nobel Peace Prize for his role in these negotiations. Indeed, for years to come one of his chief interests was to have the CIE recruit influential insiders who could help him bring home the prize.[82]

Begin's government brought sweeping change to Israel. Soon after he became prime minister, he changed the Liaison Bureau's leadership. His government transformed Israel's perception of the Jewish diaspora. Raviv and Melman write, "The new prime minister summoned Mossad chief Yitzhak Hofi and Nehemiah Levanon, who was the new head of the Liaison Bureau. . . . Begin told them that he regarded immigration to Israel as no less important than peace with Egypt [or] combating terrorism."[83] After the Soviets severed relations with Israel in 1967, it became more difficult to press for the release of Soviet Jews. Levanon believed in quiet activity, but in Israel and in the diaspora, various militant organizations were making vociferous demands for the freeing of Soviet Jewry.

Meanwhile Washington and Moscow had begun the pre-Gorbachev era of détente. Responding to American pressures, Soviet party chief Leonid Brezhnev permitted approximately 250,000 Jews to leave his country; two-thirds moved to Israel. "This increased emigration forced the Liaison Bureau to expand," Raviv and Melman write. "It began to appoint consuls to various Israeli embassies in Europe, and it sent personnel to maintain ties with Jewish organizations around the world. . . . Levanon and Mossad chief Hofi worked in close coordination on the great consensus project of immigration. . . . They knew that Prime Minister Begin wanted more."[84] Although Begin supported the Liaison Bureau's mission, he would have preferred an open and visible campaign to Levanon's secret tactics.[85]

After more than a decade as head of the Liaison Bureau, Levanon was replaced by Yehuda Lapidot, a Likud party loyalist, former hard-line Irgun militant, and talented biochemist allegedly involved with Begin in the April 1948 killing of some two hundred Arab civilians in the village of Deir Yassin near Jerusalem.[86] Israelis questioned this leadership change. Many in the diplomatic and intelligence communities, according to Raviv and Melman, "did not understand why the inexperienced Lapidot got the liaison bureau job. The new chief and Prime Minister Begin, however, understood each other perfectly. The bureau's work went much more smoothly with Lapidot happily carrying out Begin's wishes by waging a public campaign for Soviet Jewry."[87]

Despite Begin's interest in emigration and Lapidot's alacrity in managing its public dimension, Israel's policies toward Romania did not change. Jerusalem noisily demanded freedom of emigration for Soviet Jews, but it made no such demands on Romania. "Different circumstances," write Raviv and Melman, called for "different methods."[88]

General Marcu's work with Israel was not without its challenges. On June 23, 1973, his subordinate, Constantin Dumitrachescu, head of Romanian's espionage arm in Tel

Aviv, vanished from the tarmac of the Lod Airport. He had defected.

Dumitrachescu was Romania's number two man in the Tel Aviv embassy, occasionally participating in meetings with, among others, Abba Eban. After he defected, he wrote Marcu to assure him that he had no intention of damaging Romania's political regime.

DIE sent Colonel Victor Dorobantu, operating under the name of Virgil Dragomir, and General Gheorghe Bolanu to Tel Aviv to investigate Dumitrachescu's disappearance jointly with Mossad. Dorobantu and Bolinu returned to Bucharest quite empty-handed; they had uncovered only a receipt showing that Dumitrachescu had left Israel for Copenhagen.[89] Dumitrachescu's defection, though significant, was of negligible importance compared to what would follow.

In 1978 Marcu agreed with Dan on what would be his last involvement in a protocol for the emigration of Romanian Jews to Israel.[90] On July 27, 1978, a U.S. Air Force Hercules cargo plane left West Germany for Andrews Air Force Base outside of Washington with General Pacepa, deputy head of Romania's DIE, on board. Pacepa's defection shook the Romanian secret service. According to several eyewitnesses, Ceausescu became hysterical, tore off his shirt, and shouted, "I cannot even trust this shirt I am wearing!" Most of the operatives who were engaged in Romanian espionage abroad were hastily recalled. DIE agents, undercover as diplomats or as "illegals" in the West, panicked and fled.

Under the harsh and incompetent supervision of Elena Ceausescu, the president's wife, a major investigation was begun. After Pacepa's defection, the party leadership was, according to Burtica, fearful, hysterical, and suspicious.[91] The DIE collapsed.[92] In the chaotic attempt to rebuild, Pacepa determined that "twenty two ambassadors were replaced, and more than a dozen high-ranking officers were grounded while several dozen more simply vanished from sight in the turmoil."[93]

In his memoirs, Burtica writes that with the exception of several young officers, everyone in the DIE was either fired or grounded and closely investigated. For years a furious Ceausescu refused to promote ex-DIE officers to the rank of general.[94] Yet they were scapegoats; if anyone was to blame for Pacepa's defection, it was Ceausescu and his brother, General Nicolae A. Ceausescu (code named General Calin), who commanded personnel at DIE. But no one in Romania dared to blame the two brothers for their shortcomings.

As head of the U.S., Latin America, Africa, and Middle East division of DIE, General Marcu led the largest of the DIE's three services. His generals commanded several brigades.[95] Sometimes he undertook curious missions: in 1973, for example, he had to buy a rabbit leather hat for the minister of the interior, Emil Bobu, to be worn when Bobu went hunting with Ceausescu. Marcu failed on his first attempt (Bobu did not like the hat) but succeeded on the second.[96] After 1975 he controlled the *Operatiuni Valutare* (foreign currency operations), which, among other things, managed the sale of Jews to Israel and ethnic Germans to West Germany. Following Pacepa's defection, Marcu was accused by his colleagues of being a British, Soviet, and even an Israeli agent.[97]

Documents related to the investigation of Pacepa's defection indicate that Marcu adopted a reserved demeanor during the investigation. He was transferred from the DIE to another military unit, where he was marginalized as head of one of the schools for noncommissioned police officers. According to Burtica, however, in 1981 Marcu coordinated teams of Securitate officers—sent abroad on Elena Ceausescu's orders—to investigate Burtica's alleged involvement with the CIA, KGB, and Mossad.[98] When Ceausescu's reign came to an end, a retired Marcu resurfaced as a private businessman with alleged connections in London and Tehran.

After Pacepa's defection the DIE was thoroughly reorganized. Renamed the Centrul de Informatii Externe,[99] and with a force of 2,426 officers, the CIE—directly or through its militarized foreign trade companies, Dunarea and Delta—retained its essential mission: to obtain hard currency for the Ceausescu regime. The selling of Jews and ethnic Germans remained a priority.

Ceausescu plotted his own revenge against Pacepa. Under the direction of General Mot, Ceausescu commanded his newly created counterespionage unit to capture or kill the defector.[100] With Ceausescu's approval and Yasser Arafat's support, Mot enlisted the help of Carlos the Jackal, the engineer of several terrorist attacks in Europe, including the bombing of the Radio Free Europe building in Munich. Carlos received unlimited support from the Securitate, but he finally confessed to General Nicolae Plesita, head of CIE, that he could not deal with Pacepa.[101]

During the late 1970s and early 1980s, Ceausescu's political behavior became increasingly unpredictable. On the one hand he insisted that the Soviet Union participate in Middle East peace talks, and promised Israel renewed diplomatic relations with the Soviet powers.[102] On the other hand he threatened Soviet president Yuri Andropov that Romania might abandon the Warsaw Pact.[103] Ceausescu's government endorsed a peace plan with four critical points: "Israeli withdrawal from all Arab territories occupied after June 1967, including East Jerusalem and southern Lebanon; the establishment of an independent state governed by the PLO; guarantees for the security of all states in the region; and convocation of an international peace conference, with representatives from the PLO, the Soviet Union, and the United States."[104]

Although Israel rejected the plan, it continued to cultivate improved relations with Romania.[105] And it continued to buy Romanian Jews from Ceausescu. On December 31, 1982, the protocol concerning this highly confidential matter once again expired. Six months later a new, "strictly confidential" agreement was signed, valid until December 31, 1988, in which Romania promised to permit the annual "departure" to Israel of at least fifteen hundred Jews. Israel, for its part, promised to pay $3,300 for each emigré. Payments were to be made every three months.[106]

In an addendum to the agreement, however, Israel insisted that emigrés over retirement age be excluded from these arrangements. Israel did not wish to pay the ransom for them.[107] Yehuda Lapidot, head of Israel's Liaison Bureau, and Stelian Octavian Andronic, head of AVS (Aport Valutar Strain), the hard-currency unit of the CIE, signed the agreement.[108]

On February 21, 1985, Shimon Peres arrived in Bucharest as prime minister of Israel. Ceausescu again pressed for a post–Camp David mediation, which this time was to include the Soviet Union.[109] Shaike Dan briefed Peres and his adviser on the situation in Romania. Although Dan was weary of cautioning Peres about Ceausescu's greed and his repressive regime, he noted that as long as emigration continued, it was worthwhile to maintain Ceausescu's support.[110]

Dan was not the only one angry with Ceausescu and his regime; the Israeli political establishment was also losing patience. According to Ambassador Govrin, after 1985 Romania's "relations with Israel gradually deteriorated. Although the countries continued to exchange high-level visits, they failed to make major breakthroughs. Romania continued to insist on Israeli concessions, including direct negotiations with the Palestine Liberation Organization (PLO). In August 1987, Prime Minister Yitzhak Shamir of Israel, after nine hours of talks with Ceausescu in Bucharest, reported no progress on the issue of Middle East negotiations. A few months later, Ceausescu invited representatives of the PLO and the Israeli-Palestinian Dialogue Committee to a meeting in Romania, but that discussion too bore no fruit."[111]

Govrin notes that Israel was increasingly irritated by the catastrophic human rights situation in Romania. Anti-Semitism, quietly encouraged by the Romanian Communist party and openly promoted by Ceausescu's ideological henchmen, including Eugen Barbu and Corneliu Vadim Tudor, was on the rise. Articles and books denying the Holocaust were being published in an otherwise heavily censored environment. Buildings of historical significance to the Jews and old synagogues were being demolished in the "program of urban planning" personally coordinated by Ceausescu.

And while Israel's diplomatic relations with Romania tottered, Ceausescu's relations with Arafat improved. A U.S. report revealed that "Arafat and other high-ranking PLO officials frequently traveled to Bucharest. The Romanian media described Arafat as a personal friend and comrade of Ceausescu. Between November 1987 and December 1988, Arafat met with Ceausescu five times. The PLO opened one of its first diplomatic offices in Bucharest, and several bilateral agreements were concluded, some of which reportedly offered the PLO educational and even military training facilities in Romania."[112] Arafat enjoyed Bucharest. In August 1987 the Romanian Communist party received him as a head of state. He usually stayed in a CIE villa code named T16, located on Turgheniev Street very close to Ceausescu's residence.[113]

Although Ceausescu consistently supported Arafat and hired a known terrorist to do his dirty work, he did not support all Palestinian terrorist factions. Abu Nidal was welcome in Warsaw, Budapest, East Berlin, Sofia, and Belgrade, yet after killing a Jordanian diplomat, Azmial-Mufti, and wounding another in Bucharest in December 1984, Romania closed its doors to him. Nidal tried to blackmail Romania, going so far as to place bombs in its Beirut embassy. Yet Ceausescu refused to be pushed around, and Romania arrested Nidal's followers whenever possible.[114]

After the assassination of Anwar Sadat in October 1981, Ceausescu had grown worried about his own safety and left nothing to chance. He therefore improved his relationship with Arafat and condemned counterterrorist efforts by Israel and the United States. In October 1985, Romania officially condemned the Israeli raid against the PLO headquarters in Tunis, and in April 1986, Ceausescu wrote to President Reagan, condemning the U.S. attack against Libya.[115]

That same year Ceausescu's role as a mediator between Eastern bloc countries and Israel began to decline. In August, after almost twenty years of hostile silence, the Soviet Union renewed contact with Israel and generally sought to improve relations as part of its "new diplomacy."[116] Soviet satellites followed suit. Israel and Poland reestablished diplomatic relations in September 1986. Hungary improved its trade and tourism relations with Israel. And in January 1987, Israeli delegates met with Polish, Bulgarian, and Hungarian representatives to discuss agricultural cooperation.[117]

In October 1986, Prime Minister Yitzhak Shamir instructed Mossad's liaison department (not to be confused with the Liaison Bureau) to open talks with the KGB. Shamir intended to shift his attention to the release of Soviet Jews, since he felt that contacts with the Romanians were proving fruitless.[118]

Shamir's outlook was not entirely accurate. One year later, Soviet Jews emigrated to Israel via Romania, by rail and plane. Govrin recalls: "When I applied to Ceausescu in May, 1987, on behalf of Prime Minister Shamir for his permission to allow this, he gave it to me on the spot, on condition that the USSR agree to it. Indeed, the USSR accepted the idea that month. Thus the immigrants could arrive in Bucharest by a direct flight from Moscow or by train from [anywhere in] the USSR, and after a short stay there could continue by air to Israel."[119]

A Securitate report dated August 20, 1988, contains the details of this arrangement. It was agreed to verbally, but two hundred Soviet Jews had already transited through Romania. The Israeli government would pay Romania for security, for two nights' hotel accommodations in Bucharest for the emigrants, and for their airline tickets from Bucharest to Tel Aviv. According to the same document, Jordan, Tunisia, Sudan, and the Arab League pressured Bucharest to prohibit this arrangement.[120] The Romanian secret police, fearing further Arab terrorist acts on its soil, requested Ceausescu's personal advice.

When the emigration agreement expired in December 1988, a new five-year protocol was drafted the following month under Ceausescu's personal supervision. The hand-written mandate was filled with empty rhetoric and continued to use the old euphemism of the "reunification of families."[121] But Ceausescu's negotiators reached an understanding with their Israeli counterparts, and Israeli-sponsored emigration continued during 1989 together with Israeli payments to Romania.

Eleven months later, on Christmas Day, at the height of a bloody revolt, Nicolae and Elena Ceausescu were executed in Targoviste. According to Romanian media, Arab terrorists fought in defense of Ceausescu's regime; the few captured mercenaries were evacuated on a special flight to Libya. The Romanian Communist party was overthrown, and the market in Romanian Jews was closed.

6

The Money Trail

J ews, Germans, and oil are our best export commodities."[1] This was Ceausescu's estimate of Romania's foreign trade in the mid-1970s. But Romania's oil was virtually gone. It had been used by the Third Reich on the Eastern Front during World War II; its facilities had been bombed by the U.S. Air Force and the RAF; it had been taken by the Soviet Union as war reparations; and it had been consumed by the Romanian chemical industry in the manufacture of various plastics by order of Elena Ceausescu, who fancied herself a chemist. Only Jews and Germans remained. Thus did Ceausescu instruct his trusted aide, General Pacepa, to increase Romania's price tag for each Jewish or German emigrant.[2]

Before World War II more than 80 percent of Romania's foreign trade went to the West. Between 1948 and 1959, however, trade with the West dramatically declined; almost 90 percent of Romania's foreign trade shifted to Comecon nations. By far the most important trading partner during this period was the Soviet Union. Yet this was not to last.

When the Romanian Communist party began to insist on autonomous development, it brought Romania into direct conflict with the rest of the Soviet bloc. In the late 1950s and early 1960s, Khrushchev had envisioned Romania as a supplier of foodstuffs and raw materials for the more industrially developed members of Comecon. But in 1964 First Secretary Gheorghe Gheorghiu-Dej threatened to take Romania out of Comecon unless the organization recognized that each member had the right to pursue its own course of economic development.[3] Perceiving that his approach could reinforce Romania's status vis-à-vis the Soviets, Gheorghiu-Dej began to pursue alternative economic relations as early as the late 1950s. By 1964, foreign trade with Western countries was again a major source of Romanian commerce. Almost 40 percent of Romania's imports and almost a third of its exports involved the West.

When Ceausescu came to power in 1965 he adhered to the Gheorghiu-Dej program. His political vision for Romania was "independence." He needed independence from the East because he did not wish to cede political and economic control to Moscow. He needed independence too from the West in order to avoid the general inconvenience of human rights inquiries and condemnations, and of having to account for Romania's political and economic situation. He needed independence in order to build a Communist dynasty.

The West supplied Ceausescu with almost half the machinery and technology he needed to build a modern industrial base. In 1971, Romania joined the General Agreement on Tariffs and Trade (GATT), and the following year gained admission to the International Monetary Fund (IMF) and the World Bank. By 1973 roughly 47 percent of Romania's trade involved Western industrialized countries. In the process of this growth, Romania incurred an enormous trade deficit which forced it to borrow heavily from Western banks. Having temporarily quieted concerns about its human rights record, in 1975 Romania managed to secure Most Favored Nation trading status from the United States. But international disappointment with Romania returned, and by the 1980s trade relations with the West had soured.

According to a 1989 U.S. analysis, "Ceausescu blamed the IMF and 'unjustifiably high' interest rates charged by Western banks for his country's economic plight. For its part, the West charged Romania with unfair trade practices, resistance to needed economic reform, and human rights abuses."[4] Ceausescu looked elsewhere, but attempts to increase Romania's trade with less-developed countries failed. The manufacturing capacity of his potential trading partners was being swiftly diminished by oil shortages stemming from the Iran-Iraq War. Frustrated by this narrowed horizon of opportunity, Ceausescu begrudgingly resumed trade with the Soviet bloc. By 1986, socialist countries were involved in 53 percent of Romania's foreign trade. Still, Ceausescu remained defiant. He ordered his foreign trade enterprises to avoid direct relationships with business firms in other Communist countries, and he refused to take part in Comecon efforts to establish mutual convertibility of the currencies of the member states. Yet despite these attempts to follow an independent path, Romania lost its Most Favored Nation status in 1988, and shortly thereafter it failed to negotiate a new trade agreement with the European Economic Community (EEC).

A Stalinist economically and politically, Ceausescu's appetite for independence was as great as his thirst for hard currency—the ticket, he believed, to economic stability. He supported major industrial failures in a botched attempt to become an international economic force; stationed Romanian diplomats and spies abroad to keep a watchful eye on the Western world, hoping to steal its military and technological secrets; and tried, albeit backwardly, to modernize his own country.

For Ceausescu, the thought of independence was sweeter even than national strength and prosperity; his political strategy for realizing it proved to be catastrophic. Beginning in 1984, Romania sought no further loans from the IMF or the World Bank, curtailed imports from hard-currency nations, and maximized exports. Although the Romanian standard of living plummeted, the country generated trade surpluses as large as $2 billion a year through the rest of the decade. In April 1989, with great fanfare, Ceausescu announced the retirement of the foreign debt, declaring that Romania had at last achieved full economic and political independence.[5]

In fact he had run the country into the ground. In 1989 Romania was second only to Albania as the poorest Communist nation in Europe. The general population was daily confronted with shortages of food and energy. In a country with a predominantly agricultural economy, basic foodstuffs such as cooking oil, sugar, and salami could be purchased only with government coupons, which allocated a quota to each Romanian citizen.

In the 1960s, small co-ops had commonly sprung up here and there in East European Communist countries, especially in Poland and Hungary but also in Romania. They contained shoe shops and tailors, family restaurants and coffeehouses. Yet the most important co-op in Romania's economy was not in the business of hemming a trouser leg or baking warm pretzels; the foreign intelligence branch of the secret police was in the business of selling Jews and Germans.

The DGIE wanted hard currency, and this was not simply a matter of following orders. Incentives were also involved. The decisions of Romania's Council of Ministers allowed the Romanian Ministry of the Interior and especially the DGIE to retain part of the hard currency they earned from exports. According to a February 23, 1966, directive, the DGIE was to give 80 percent of its export earnings to the Romanian treasury; it could keep the remainder.[6]

The DGIE's role in obtaining hard currency was not Ceausescu's invention but that of his predecessor, Gheorghiu-Dej. As we have seen, because of the Jacober operation, and with the help of the Liaison Bureau, the DGIE came to manage the most modern agricultural system in Romania. By the mid-1960s that operation netted between $8 million and $10 million annually. It was deposited by the DGIE in a secret bank account accessible only by Gheorghiu-Dej.[7]

Reflecting on the changes in Romanian government that were instituted by Ceausescu, General Pacepa writes: "he reorganized the DGIE, increasing its size from 700 to 2,800 officers and raising its foreign currency budget eightfold. After that the DGIE's main task was to lay hands on as much Western money as it could, to support Romania's bankrupt economy. How was not important, only how much. . . . One of the ways to do that was in smuggling operations. Drugs confiscated at the Romanian borders and unmarked arms were turned over to the DGIE's new, supersecret 'OV' [Operatiuni Valutare] section. Trading prospective emigrés for hard currency became another of the DIE's main jobs. . . . The cruel truth is that virtually 90 percent of the Romanian citizens who emigrated to the West in the 1970s were secretly ransomed in foreign currency by either Israel or West Germany, or by their own relatives in the West."[8]

Ceausescu viewed the DGIE (and its successors, the DIE and the CIE) as one of Romania's major foreign currency providers. According to Liviu Turcu, the Securitate's tasks related to foreign trade were so important to its leadership that when its head, Tudor Postelnicu, was promoted to minister of the interior, he retained oversight of this revenue-producing responsibility and reported directly to Ceausescu. His successor, General Iulian Vlad, declared in March 1990 that the entire Securitate and Ministry of the Interior worked for a military foreign-trade enterprise, ICE Dunarea.

In spite of Dej's initial orders prohibiting a direct trade in human beings, cash receipts from such sales remained lively and profits continued to accumulate. Alexandru Draghici, a former Politburo member and minister of internal affairs, declared during a 1969 investigation into his office: "When I left the Ministry of the Interior [in July 1965], I deposited into an account of the Bank of Romania $6,250,000 from the people who were leaving the country. . . . I reported to the party leadership about it then and later."[9] When asked why some people left Romania without paying, Draghici responded, "Most of them were old Jews. In fact, Israel was paying, but it was not only an Israeli problem. There were some self-appointed intermediaries abroad who were offering amounts of money for x or y. I reported to the leadership about this and I had approval in this direction."[10]

Bartering Jews or selling them directly was not the only way in which Romania obtained money from Israel. Commercial trade between the two countries was also used by Romanian Communist authorities to extort cash from Israel against the emigration of the Jews.

During the barter period, yearly cash deposits in favor of the Romanian government were made by Israel in exchange for the emigration of the Jews. During the early 1960s, when Romania's exports to Israel were weaker than Israeli exports to Romania, cash paid by Israel was used to balance the trade between the two countries. A document stamped "strictly secret" and dated November 23, 1961 (the original document was destroyed roughly ten months later), describes one of these yearly cash payments: "In 1960 lumber exports [from Romania] to Israel stopped, though Israel insisted on this product. Consequently the trade balance in favor of the People's Republic of Romania suffered. Romania's commercial account nonetheless remained rather considerable because of the sum of 4.7 million rubles (about $1.2 million) originating from noncommercial revenues."[11]

More or less the same situation prevailed in the following year. The same report notes that on September 30, 1961, a Romanian account in the Bank of Israel contained $900,000, a sum originating again from *"noncommercial revenues"* [italics in original].[12]

Another secret report from the Ministry of Foreign Affairs clarifies the meaning of "noncommercial revenues." The report notes that in 1961, 12,150 people were allowed to emigrate to Israel. The report also states that in 1960

Romania exported goods valued at $1 million to Israel, and imported goods valued at $2.2 million. "The exchange can be considered balanced, taking into account the sum of over one million dollars which rests at the Bank of Israel in a Romanian account. The sum originates from noncommercial income related to the expenses of those who leave for Israel."[13] Similar accountings for 1962 and 1967 show continuing trade deficits that are "corrected" in Romania's favor by the same "noncommercial income." More precisely, the selling of the Romanian Jews became part of the trade balance between the two countries.

Over a year's time, Romania often exported goods to Israel that were not always needed by the Jewish state, in sum producing roughly twice the value of Israeli exports to Romania. At the end of each year Israel would pay Romania the difference in cash. It can be safely assumed that these arrangements continued until 1989, as Ambassador Govrin notes in his memoirs: "Israel's trade with Romania [continued between] 1985 and 1989 on a principle agreed to [in 1984] by Israel's minister of industry and trade, Gideon Pat, and his Romanian counterpart in Bucharest—according to which Israel would import goods from Romania at a volume twice that of goods exported by Israel to Romania. This was an Israeli gesture."[14] According to Raviv and Melman, "The Jewish State imported far more Romanian goods than it truly needed—as there is a limit to how much prune jam a country can use."[15]

In fact, a jar of Romanian prune jam could sell in Israel for the price of an empty glass jar. The Israeli government would sometimes instruct state-owned agencies to do business with Romania even if the deal was unprofitable. Take, for example, negotiations between the Romanian foreign

trade company Industrial Export and the Israeli transportation company ZIM. ZIM needed four maritime freighters.
According to the Romanian ambassador, V. Georgescu,
ZIM's director confessed to him that he had instructions
from the Israeli government not to acquire these ships from
Yugoslavian or Norwegian companies that were offering
them at lower prices. They should be bought from Romania because of "special interests" that superseded commercial ones.[16]

Ceausescu's Romania had other incentives for develop-
ing economic relations with Israel. They enabled Romania
to obtain credits in hard currency under highly advantageous conditions. According to records from the Romanian
Ministry of Foreign Affairs, in 1970 Israel granted a $7 mil-
lion loan to Romania without interest. Since these kinds of
"loans" can rarely be found, it is likely that either Israel or
a major American Jewish fund-raising organization paid the
interest. This was not the only occurrence of such a loan. A
former high-ranking official at the Israeli Ministry of Foreign Affairs told the author that Israel obtained loans for the
Romanian government from West German banks, then
paid the interest. According to Pacepa, Romania received
"several additional large credits issued by various Western
banks, with part of the interest payments defrayed by Yeshahanu [Shaike Dan]."[17]

Romanian authorities also obtained hard currency
through preferential exchange rates offered by major Jewish
organizations in the United States that wished to support a
Romanian welfare program—organized by the Federation
of Romanian Jewish Communities—for needy and old Jews.

In 1964, Romanian authorities admitted the Joint
back into Romania. As Rabbi Rosen recalls: "I warned the

government that the Joint was using excuses not to begin work in Romania, and that the Romanians had to take the initiative in breaking the impasse. They responded by agreeing to an exchange rate for the dollar which was 25 percent higher than normal, but they insisted that an agreement could be signed only if I brought in $200,000 a year. I traveled to the United States and managed to obtain $600,000. As a result, the Romanian authorities agreed to a rate of 15 *lei* to the dollar. This was 25 percent more than the official rate for gifts, which was 12 *lei*. The general official rate was 6 *lei* per dollar. The Joint wanted a rate of 18 *lei*, so the haggling continued. It took three long years before we could come to a satisfactory arrangement with the Joint."[18] The rate eventually obtained by Rosen was at least three times higher than the market exchange rate. Even the so-called advantageous rate obtained by the Joint allowed the DGIE to cash a good deal of hard currency: under the Communist regime the worthless *leu* was always heavily overrated compared to the dollar.

When Ceausescu took power, he virtually halted the barter system of Jews for agricultural products. He wanted cash, and the Israeli government provided it for every Romanian Jew that reached Lod Airport to begin the absorption program. The Dan-Marcu agreements, periodically reviewed by both sides, regularly filled Romania's treasury. General Pacepa writes: "In July 1978 this payment amounted to between $2,000 and $50,000 per person. Sometimes Yeshahanu [Dan] was asked to pay up to $250,000."[19] Marcu brought Dan lists of Jews approved for emigration, and Dan and Yanai brought suitcases of cash. It was in 1974 that one of these suitcases, containing $1 million, was lost in Zurich's airport, only to be found intact two days later.

Although Israeli authorities generally paid $2,000 for each Jew who emigrated from Romania to Israel, Romanian authorities asked for as much as $250,000 in "special cases." Lazar Derera, a Romanian foreign trade employee of Jewish origin, was arrested by Romanian authorities for allegedly sabotaging the economy in a deal with the Tel Aviv–based company Chemical Phosphate. According to Phyllis Yadin, Jacober tried unsuccessfully in 1972 to obtain Derera's release for a quarter of a million dollars.[20]

A former high-ranking functionary of the Israeli Ministry of Foreign Affairs reports that the 1983 negotiations for renewal of the emigration agreement were particularly nettlesome. Ceausescu had decreed that all would-be emigrants must repay the expense of the free education they had received in Romania's schools. And CIE negotiators demanded $600,000 in return for Romania's agreeing to exceed the annual emigration limit of two thousand Jews. To Romania's annoyance, the Israelis consistently refused to pay for small children and retirees. Israel, for its part, pointed to Romania's deception with respect to the education of its emigrants: often a low-ranking technician was sold as an engineer with an advanced degree. The CIE demanded $9,500 for each Jew and $15,500 for those between the ages of sixteen and sixty who had educational credentials, from a high school diploma to a Ph.D.

In 1989 the Romanians reiterated that the price for each Jewish emigrant must be raised in compensation for the cost of that person's education and health care. Romanian representatives also requested that Israel be willing to accept fewer than its annual minimum quota of emigrants, and they demanded that Israel pay in advance for the emigrants' transportation to Israel. According to a high-ranking former Israeli diplomat, the Romanians were paid by the Jewish Agency with funds that originated usually from the United Jewish Appeal, sometimes from the American Joint Distribution Committee (the Joint) in the United States.

Ceausescu personally supervised the DIE's financial operations. By the close of 1973 he had opened a secret account that he controlled personally, code named TA, which contained every penny obtained by the DIE from its foreign currency operations. According to Pacepa, "The money the DIE obtained from the West in the form of checks or bank transfers that could be legally controlled was immediately deposited in the Romanian bank of foreign trade known as BRCE and credited to the national budget. But the money obtained by the DIE in hard cash—most of it from the export of Jews and Germans—was recorded only in Ceausescu's TA accounts. Cash received in other currencies was exchanged in dollars, usually in Zurich. The dollar bills received from Bonn and Tel Aviv were first 'laundered' into new ones in case the numbers were recorded, and then were kept in a DIE underground vault. This was Ceausescu's secret slush fund."[21]

Propelled by a thirst for hard currency, in 1970 Ceausescu and Ion Stanescu (head of Securitate) ordered the DIE to begin Peregrinii (Pilgrims), another extortion operation related to emigration. It was coordinated by General Gheorghe Bolanu, head of the DIE's third division (which controlled emigration and counterespionage), and General Eugen Luchian, who served in the Office for Security and Military Matters of the Romanian government. Romanian citizens with relatives who wished to leave the country, or potential candidates themselves—whether ethnic Romanians, Germans, or Jews—were approached and asked for cash, apartments in Romania, cars, and other valuables in exchange for permission to emigrate. The going rate was $826 to $10,000 per person.

In December 1973, Ceausescu terminated Peregrinii under the pretext of "unfavorable echoes in the international media."[22] But in fact the reason was that too many DIE officers and informants—dealing privately with emigrants—were diverting funds from Ceausescu's pockets.[23] In its first seven months, Peregrinii netted slightly more than $1.3 million in deutschemarks, French francs, and Swiss francs.[24] Investigated after Pacepa's 1978 defection, General Luchian stated that Peregrinii generated a total of about $6 million for Romania's treasury.

According to Pacepa, the unit charged with securing cash from the West and administering the funds obtained from the sale of Jews also constructed and managed a factory that produced synthetic diamonds based on technologies stolen from the De Beers company of South Africa, and using equipment illegally imported from Sweden. The DIE unit also managed two Romanian foreign trade companies, one specializing in contraband arms and industrial diamonds, the other in civil and industrial construction in the Third World.[25] Pacepa recalls, "Obtaining cash dollars from the West had taken priority over all the DIE's other intelligence jobs. [In 1978] Ceausescu increased the DIE's annual quota to $1 billion. Of course the DIE was far from being in a position to meet such a ridiculous quota."[26]

In the spring of 1978, Ceausescu widened his command of the DIE's hard-currency operations. He took control of the DIE's bank accounts by creating a "collecting account" code named OV-78. Signed by Teodor Coman, minister of the interior, the order creating account OV-78—which contained $64,761,473—stated that it was created by Ceausescu's order. It also stated that money kept in accounts TN-73 and TN-75, which held funds obtained from the sale of Jews and ethnic Germans, should be transferred to OV-78. Lastly, it ordered the DIE to double OV-78's balance. This order was to be handled by Generals Pacepa, Alexandru Danescu, Gheorghe Marcu, and Teodor Sirbu.[27]

How was the DIE to achieve these goals? An appendix to the same order specified traditional export operations in addition to the "confidential export of neutralized goods," the "selling of products prohibited for export or import," and the "selling of weapons, ammunition, and military equipment."[28] The "confidential export of neutralized goods" meant that a country's import quotas would be circumvented by using a third party with access to that market. The "selling of products prohibited for export or import" meant, according to Pacepa, that the DIE should obtain hard currency from the sale of counterfeited Kent cigarettes, Teacher's Scotch whiskey, and Campari aperitif, all manufactured illegally in Romania under the DIE's supervision.

Ceausescu also authorized the DIE to sell drugs to the West. He used his own border patrol and counterfeited documents in order to profit from the drug trade. In one episode related by Pacepa, Ceausescu "had just been informed that three hundred pounds of cocaine from the Middle East had been confiscated at the Romanian border on its way to the West, and he had ordered his minister of the interior to draw up false documents showing that the cocaine had been burned in accordance with international agreements Romania had signed. 'The West needs oxygen, doesn't it?' Ceausescu quipped, looking at Doicaru and me. The money the DIE obtained from smuggling that cocaine into Western Europe added a healthy padding to Ceausescu's special 'TA' bank account."[29]

When it came to the sale of weapons, ammunition, and military equipment, Ceausescu had no scruples. Using the Romanian Defense Ministry's foreign trade company, Romtehnica, he sold weapons to whoever was interested. In 1985, according to the *Washington Post*, Romania was the world's fifth-largest exporter of munitions.[30] It sold any kind of weapon its DIE officers could steal or its industry could reproduce. It sold uniforms to Saddam Hussein during the Iran-Iraq War and jointly entered into military manufacturing ventures with Muammar Gadhafi. It even sold Soviet military technology to the U.S. government. In July 1979, Washington purchased four personnel carriers from Ceausescu via his brothers Marin and Ilie. The former was stationed as a commercial attaché in Vienna while the latter served as Romania's deputy minister of defense. Designed to be used for training purposes, with a "low level of sophistication," according to correspondent Benjamin Weiser, the vehicles arrived in the United States "on a Yugoslav freighter, the *Klek*."[31]

The four personnel carriers had no special value for Washington, but this was the beginning of an astonishing relationship. Weiser writes, "For ten years before deposed Romanian dictator Nicolae Ceausescu's execution, the U.S. government secretly bought advanced military technology from Romania. . . . As a part of the clandestine intelligence program coordinated by the CIA, the U.S. government paid more than $40 million through foreign middlemen, with about 20 percent ending up in Swiss accounts controlled by the Ceausescu family. . . . The U.S. military were able to obtain important components of tactical, non-nuclear weaponry—including air defense systems—that the Soviet Union has in place to protect itself and other Warsaw Pact countries. From Romania alone the acquisitions included the latest version of the Shilka, one of the most effective anti-aircraft systems in the Soviet inventory; mobile rocket launchers that had been modified and improved by the Romanian military; and radar systems used in identifying and directing. . . . Of all the East Bloc deals, the Romanian transactions may have been the most stunning because of Ceausescu's involvement."[32]

As in all Communist countries, Romania's economic and social bureaucracy was notoriously inefficient and corrupt. Yet when it came to the hard-currency operations, business was streamlined. According to Liviu Turcu, head of the North America department of the CIE, who defected to the United States in January 1989, "In order to organize the special hard currency operations, at the beginning of the 1980s, on Nicolae Ceausescu's secret order no. 000320, a special structure was created in CIE, its existence a secret even inside the [Romanian foreign intelligence]. Named U.M. 0107/AVS, this structure had discretionary authority inside the Securitate over foreign trade operations."[33]

This special unit of the CIE was headed by Colonel Stelian Octavian Andronic and later by Lieutenant Colonel Constantin Anghelache. Andronic and Anghelache replaced Marcu, and handled the sale of Romanian Jews to the Israeli Liaison Bureau.

A former DIE officer stationed in Israel and the Netherlands, Andronic was trusted by the Securitate's leaders and by Ceausescu personally since he had been involved in the ultra-sensitive sale of weapons to the United States. According to Weiser, beginning in 1979 Andronic "flew to Switzerland on a regular basis and coordinated the diversion of funds to the family's secret bank accounts . . . and . . . sometimes opened the accounts himself."[34]

Andronic later explained that his mission involved "the following main tasks: to bring to Romania hard currency resulting from the estates of Romanians who lived abroad; to transfer to special accounts from the BRCE . . . the amounts that resulted from the agreements with West Germany and Israel concerning emigration; to handle the operations for obtaining hard currency apart from the export of goods; and to obtain commissions from various foreign trade operations."[35]

According to Leibovici-Lais, in the late 1960s the West German government probably discovered that Romania was selling its Jews to Israel. One way or another, the Romanians suggested to the Germans that the two countries begin to discuss the emigration of ethnic Germans from Romania. "But, from habit, they imposed one condition: keep this a secret, and don't tell the Israelis anything."[36]

The West German government defied Romania's caution and queried the Israeli government directly. According to Shaike Dan, "On more than one occasion our ambassador in Bonn, Arthur Ben-Nathan, was asked by ministers in the German government how Israel manages to get the Jews out of Romania. Golda Meir was even asked to come and explain it."[37]

In 1967, when diplomatic relations between Romania and West Germany were first established, "roughly 60,000 ethnic Germans requested permission to emigrate." According to the same U.S. report, by 1978 "some 80,000 had departed for West Germany."[38] Ceausescu's sale of ethnic Germans to West Germany was no different from his sale of Jews to Israel: "In 1978 the two countries negotiated an agreement concerning the remaining German population, which had decreased from 2 percent of the total population in 1966 to 1.6 percent in 1977. Romania agreed to allow 11,000 to 13,000 ethnic Germans to emigrate each year in return for hard currency and a payment of 5,000 deutschemarks [$2,414] per person [under the pretext] of reimbursing the state for educational expenses. In 1982 that figure rose to $3,122–$3,568 [7,000–8,000 deutschemarks] per person. In the decade between 1978 and 1988, approximately 120,000 Germans emigrated, leaving behind a population of only about 200,000, between 80 and 90 percent of whom wanted to emigrate. . . . In 1987 an entire village of some 200 ethnic Germans applied *en masse* for emigration permits."[39]

As with the sale of Jews to Israel, Romania obtained loans without interest from West Germany in exchange for its ethnic Germans. The negotiations, however, were fraught with challenges. In 1979, West Germany's chancellor Helmut Schmidt visited Bucharest and "extended credit guarantees of approximately $368 million in return for Romanian pledges to facilitate the reunification of ethnic German families."[40] In 1983 the question of emigration was again discussed as Ceausescu sought to increase the "education tax" per ethnic German emigrant from the equivalent of $2,632 to $42,105. Both Bavarian premier Franz Joseph Strauss and West German foreign minister Hans-Dietrich Genscher visited Romania and agreed to pay approximately

$5,263 per emigrant. According to press reports, the agreement remained in effect through June 1988 and provided for the annual emigration of 11,000 to 13,000 Transylvanian Saxons. In January 1989, Romania agreed to maintain this rate of emigration.

Romania's relations with West Germany—at their most cordial during Willi Brandt's chancellorship—deteriorated in the 1980s. In a 1984 visit to Bonn, Ceausescu sought to exploit a setback in West German relations with Bulgaria, East Germany, and the Soviet Union. Observers believed the Romanian president was determined to rebuild his reputation in the West. But disagreements over arms control, trade, and the treatment of ethnic Germans darkened the talks and prevented Ceausescu from gaining ground.

In the late 1980s, as West Germany lost patience with Romanian policies, restrained criticism gave way to outright protest. In April 1989, Chancellor Helmut Kohl declared that the situation of Romania's ethnic Germans had become intolerable. The West German Foreign Ministry officially condemned Romania's human rights policies.[41]

Edgar Hirt, West Germany's chief "reunification of families" negotiator with East Germany, declared that Romania's primary negotiation tactic was blackmail. "The Romanians had proved quite cash-thirsty indeed. Entire families of ethnic Germans seeking to emigrate and claim German citizenship had sometimes been arrested by the Securitate, the secret police arm of the most ruthless dictatorship the Communist world had known since Stalin's death."

Hirt's protests against the Romanian government's practices had little effect. According to Romanian officials, Bonn willingly sponsored the liberation of East German political prisoners. Interested in liberating Germans from

Romania, Hirt made direct payments to the Romanian diplomats and DIE undercover officers stationed in Bonn. According to Craig Whitney, an expert in the history of the East German secret services, "Hirt began inviting the [Romanian] ambassador or his deputy chief of mission for a chat and a cup of coffee, sometimes, he claimed, wordlessly slipping an envelope with 50,000 or 60,000 deutschemarks [$18,000–$21,000] across the table. Freed with money thus drawn from [the Catholic church's] Caritas, the arrested ethnic Germans began to turn up at Frankfurt airport."[42]

Ceausescu also attempted to extort money from West Germany by using the tens of thousands of Holocaust victims who still lived in Romania. He wanted the war reparations owed to the Jewish and Romanian victims to be placed in his own bank accounts, whereupon he would pay the victims in *lei* at an exchange rate he established. According to the West German ambassador Erwin Wickert, who served in Romania between 1971 and 1976, "The German side refused systematically to take into account these requests under the pretext that Romania under Antonescu was an ally of Nazi Germany. At Ceausescu's order, faked lists of victims were given to Germany. During his visit in Bonn, the Romanian dictator tried once more—without success—to play the restitution card."[43] According to a former Israeli diplomat, the Romanian authorities enlisted Moses Rosen in an effort to obtain these reparations from Germany, but Israel opposed this deal and it fell through.

Wickert notes in his memoirs the amounts paid for various German immigrants: 1,800 deutschemarks ($650) for a person with no education; 5,500 deutschemarks ($1,964) for a university student; 7,000 deutschemarks ($2,500) for a student in the final year of school; 11,000 deutschemarks

($3,298) for a person with an M.A. or M.B. degree; and 2,900 deutschemarks ($1,035) for a skilled worker. He also describes how the money changed hands: Securitate officers traveling to Germany picked up the cash and carried it in suitcases direct to Switzerland, where they deposited it in secret accounts.[44]

According to a 1991 memo addressed by the Romanian minister of foreign affairs to his colleague in the Ministry of Justice, these German funds were "deposited in a Swiss bank in Basel in [one of] two accounts. One of the accounts was open to Romanian companies, but the other was known only by those who made the payments and by the people trusted by the Ceausescu family."[45]

Germany not only paid for the emigrants but, in December 1983 or January 1984, deposited an additional 1 million deutschemarks ($421,230) in a CIE account. "The Germans' condition was that Romania use this money to buy only German products. Ceausescu obliged . . . and bought 'special equipment' for the Romanian ministry of the interior." In 1982 the West German government also offered Romania a low-interest credit of 800 million deutschemarks ($330 million).[46]

For 22 years, Dr. Heinz Guenther Huesch mediated on behalf of West Germany with the DIE and CIE. According to the Canadian Broadcasting Company, over the course of 200 meetings Huesch negotiated about 200,000 departures of ethnic Germans from Romania at a price of 10,000 to 15,000 deutschemarks ($4,000 to $6000) per person.[47] For years, according to Pacepa, Huesch was Marcu's main contact, which Ceausescu "considered potentially even more advantageous," given that there was now a far greater population of ethnic Germans in Romania than Jews.[48]

West German emigration payments to Romania were largely made by Commerzbank AG-Neuss. A Romanian investigation into Ceausescu's foreign bank accounts—begun after his execution—revealed that AG-Neuss made payments to the BRCE accounts OV-78, Feroviarul, AA, and AC—all of which were CIE accounts controlled by Ceausescu. AG-Neuss made a total of thirteen payments with a combined value of more than 134 million deutschemarks (about $54 million).[49] As recently as August 24, 1989, four months before Ceausescu's execution, Huesch had AG-Neuss pay Lieutenant Colonel Anghelache, Colonel Andronic's successor in the handling of these accounts, 9,308,000 deutschemarks (about $5 million).[50]

Israel also fattened Ceausescu's accounts. Indeed, according to a Canadian investigative journalist, the Israeli government and Jewish organizations had paid Ceausescu no less than $60 million in cash in return for Jewish exit visas in the 1970s and 1980s.[51] At one point in the mid-1980s Shaike Dan obtained from the Joint an extra $250,000 (beyond the moneys regularly paid to the Israeli authorities by the Jewish Agency for the emigration of Romanian Jews), which he paid to his Romanian contacts in order to obtain exit visas for an additional eight hundred Jews.[52] A high-ranking former Israeli diplomat estimated that $50 million was paid by the Israeli government to DIE/CIE for exit visas. A rough calculation would indicate that, between 1968 and 1989, Ceausescu sold 40,577 Jews to Israel for $112,498,800, at a price of $2,500 and later at $3,300 per head.

Israel actually paid less per head for emigration than the amounts noted above, since it paid for neither children nor retirees. An accurate accounting must nonetheless include the money given to Romania during the barter periods (these amounts are difficult to estimate) as well as the funds conveyed each year by Israel to cover the import-export difference between the two countries. Pacepa's generalization is probably the most accurate: "Over the years the Yeshahanu [Dan]-Marcu agreement netted Bucharest hundreds of millions of dollars."

The Jewish minority in Romania declined dramatically because of emigration. By 1988 the Jewish population there had dwindled to roughly 23,000, of which half were sixty-five or older.[53] Consequently Romanian authorities had to scramble to find enough Romanian Jews to fill their promised quota. In 1989, Ceausescu directed the CIE to allow people in mixed marriages to leave for Israel, and to obtain more money per head.[54] It is unknown whether a final emigration agreement was signed in the second half of 1989. In that year, 941 Romanian Jews left for Israel, and Bank Leumi deposited $3.2 million in four installments into the TN-75 account controlled by Ceausescu and the AA account controlled by Securitate. That same year the New York Bank Hapoalim deposited another $2 million to the same AA account of BRCE.[55]

In December 1989, during the trial of Ceausescu and his wife Elena, the prosecutor asked, "Let us now talk about the accounts in Switzerland, Mr. Ceausescu. What about the accounts?" Elena Ceausescu replied, "Accounts in Switzerland? Furnish proof!" Ceausescu said, "We had no account in Switzerland. Nobody has opened an account. This shows again how false the charges are. What defamation, what provocation!"[56] Three hours later a firing squad executed the Ceausescus.

In 1990 the former minister of the interior, Tudor Poștelnicu, was imprisoned along with the members of the Romanian Communist party Politburo. But Lieutenant Colonel Anghelache, allegedly his nephew, whom Dan Badea, a gifted Romanian journalist, called "a doctor in the slave trade," was still at large, slipping over borders under false names and various passports, hastily closing accounts and transferring Ceausescu's fortune to new ones. His role as Romania's delegate to the FIFA (the International Federation of Football Associations—the most important world soccer association) was, according to Liviu Turcu, the perfect cover for his travels to Switzerland's banks.[57]

7

The Washington Equation

When Ceausescu came to power, Romania's relations with the United States were cool and peripheral. Although Romania's condemnation of the Warsaw Pact invasion of Czechoslovakia and the opening of the Vietnam War–related Paris peace talks improved the atmosphere, U.S. trade restrictions with Eastern European countries held economic relations to a minimum. Then, in August 1969, President Nixon visited Romania—the first visit to a Communist country by an American head of state since the 1945 Yalta Conference. Nixon was warmly received. He and Ceausescu discussed a wide variety of international problems and agreed, as a U.S. embassy report noted, "upon the mutual establishment of libraries, the opening of negotiations for the conclusion of a consular convention, and the development and diversification of economic ties."[1] Nixon sought to improve economic relations with Romania, and in 1972 Congress debated granting the country Most Favored Nation status.

David Funderburk, a former ambassador to Romania, observed that Ceausescu and Nixon were "admiring friends" because they had "such a fixation on power—its acquisition and retention," and because "Nixon and Kissinger apparently became convinced that Ceausescu could be trusted and was a bona fide maverick. Thus they could use him. In reality he has used them."[2] Nixon's spectacular overture to Romania set a precedent that many succeeding administrations in Washington would follow.

One of the main goals of Ceausescu's foreign policy, for reasons of trade and prestige, was to obtain Most Favored Nation status. But the goodwill of U.S. administrations, Ceausescu's diplomatic gimmicks, and the efforts of his Ministry of Foreign Affairs (dominated by DIE officers) fell short of their target.

To obtain Most Favored Nation status, the U.S. Congress had to be persuaded to grant it. Toward this end Ceausescu enlisted the help of Rabbi Rosen and the Israeli government. Rosen described his lobbying efforts: "Beginning in 1975 . . . I ceaselessly strove to obtain this U.S. status for Romania. It would provide the country with many hundreds of millions of dollars, on the one hand; it would also facilitate *alyah*, i.e., the possibility for every Jew to leave for Israel if he wished to do so."[3]

Govrin confirms Rosen and Israel's efforts to help Romania. Rosen, he writes, "served as an advocate for Romania's leadership among the American administration and [in] public opinion by praising the freedom of religious observances and the national rights that the Jews enjoyed in Romania. Israel's prime ministers and ambassadors in Washington and Bucharest joined Chief Rabbi Rosen's activity as intercessor, as did Jewish organizations in the U.S.A., which were impressed by the relative liberty exercised by Romania's Jewish minority. . . . They also took into consideration Romania's policy of permitting Jews to emigrate to Israel (though not at the desired rate); that it had not broken off diplomatic relations with Israel; the fact that Romania did not vote for the anti-Zionist resolution in the United Nations; and its enabling free access (although always monitored by the security service) of official Israeli representatives in Bucharest to maintain contact with Romania's Jewish communities."[4]

Israel was initially reluctant to support Romania's bid for Most Favored Nation status, but Ceausescu threatened to halt the emigration of Romanian Jews without Israeli support. The Israeli agencies in charge of emigration and the Israeli cabinet met to discuss this situation. They hesitated. Ceausescu sent Rosen to Israel with the message, "Help us obtain the MFN, otherwise Romanian Jews will starve"—an implicit threat to the Joint's operation in Romania.

Despite reservations about Rosen, Israel eventually decided to support Romania's bid for Most Favored Nation status. Yet its support made a negligible impact on the emigration of Jews from Romania.[5] Rosen knew that Israel held him in low esteem: "Certain interests in Israel were unhappy with some of my initiatives. This occurred in particular during my prolonged efforts to help the Romanian economy by using the goodwill that I had obtained in the United States."[6]

Ambassador Roger Kirk, who represented the United States in Romania between 1984 and 1989, and Mircea Raceanu, head of the U.S. desk in Romania's Ministry of Foreign Affairs, assessed Rosen's lobbying efforts: "Rosen's consummate skill [was] at operating within the Romanian system and [in] his willingness to be useful to Ceausescu by lobbying for Romania in the United States and by issuing public statements of gratitude to Ceausescu's Jewish policy even while pushing Ceausescu for additional concessions. Rosen's maneuverings and self-importance . . . earned him the enmity, even contempt, of some observers inside and outside Romania. Others considered his service to Ceausescu as a betrayal of his honor and even of his faith."[7] Kirk and Raceanu believe that Rosen sincerely tried to help his people, and that he was effective precisely because he was uncompromising.

With Rosen and Israel's assistance, Ceausescu finally prevailed. In July 1975 the U.S. Congress approved the entire Romanian trade package and renewed Most Favored Nation status beginning in January 1976.[8] Ceausescu was jubilant and believed, according to Kirk, that Washington "needed Romania so badly that it would grant him MFN status without the conditions mandated by U.S. law."[9]

This miscalculation would later cost Ceausescu dearly. As Govrin writes, "Romania enjoyed this status in conjunction with the Jackson-Vanik Amendment passed by the American Congress as an integral part of the Trade Law, stipulating that the granting of MFN status to Communist countries should be conditional upon granting of permission to emigrate to its citizens."[10] Furthermore, Congress was to reassess the status annually. Ceausescu had opened Romania to periodic scrutiny from abroad; his unwillingness to improve local human rights conditions would lead to conflict.

In 1975, as Kirk writes, Romania became the first East European country to receive Most Favored Nation status; by 1981 bilateral trade had reached $1 billion. Yet because of "persistent reports of human rights violations in Romania and the regime's decision to impose an education tax on applicants for exit visas, the United States Congress hesitated to renew most-favored-nation status."[11] Major Jewish organizations in the United States became suspicious of Ceausescu's actions. The Romanian dictator allowed 2,393 Jews to leave for Israel in 1975 and 2,223 in 1976, far below 1973 and 1974 numbers when 4,123 and 3,729 respectively were allowed to leave. In 1977, in an effort to boost emigration numbers, Dr. William Korey from B'nai B'rith International and Jacob Birnbaum of the Center for Russian and East European Jewry "urged Congress to implement a monitoring procedure to facilitate Jewish emigration."[12]

On April 12, 1978, President Jimmy Carter cordially greeted Ceausescu in Washington but emphasized the importance of human rights in bilateral relations. The next day Ceausescu met with Senator Henry "Scoop" Jackson at the Romanian embassy. According to Pacepa, in his discussion with Ceausescu "Jackson was polite but very firm, his main concern being over human rights and freedom of emigration. He stated flatly that, based on his experience, Bucharest repeatedly tried to cheat on emigration; that the current situation, according to verifiable figures he had, was far from satisfactory; that emigration policies and human rights were systematically violated by Bucharest; and that substantial corrections would have to be made if Romania wanted to preserve its most-favored-nation status."[13] Nestor Rates, the Washington correspondent for Radio Free Europe, recalled that, having listened to Ceausescu, Jackson closed the meeting by saying: "Mr. President, [what you have said] is propaganda. No emigration, no MFN."[14]

Israel, not wishing to jeopardize the influx of Jews from Romania, had worried that if Romania were granted Most Favored Nation status, Washington would eventually discover its special emigration arrangements. According to Rosen, "Certain circles in Israel were actually conducting an organized campaign against granting MFN status to Romania."[15] No one in the United States knew what was happening, according to Pacepa, until he defected. Even President Carter was unaware of the deal between Israel and Romania; he noted on Pacepa's report of the arrangement, "Absolute novelty."[16]

Jewish organizations in the United States were also divided over the renewal of Romania's Most Favored Nation status. In 1979, Jacob Birnbaum, a crusader for Soviet Jewry, "wanted Congress to suspend . . . the MFN until Romania increased the number of Jews permitted to emigrate to Israel."[17] The Conference of Presidents of Major American Jewish Organizations, on the other hand, endorsed the extension. In Rosen's view, "The leaders of the pro-Israel lobby in Washington were involved in a sophisticated campaign. They did not ask that the MFN status be withheld from Romania, but that the possibility should always be there so that the Romanians should be frightened into agreeing to increase the number of Jews leaving for Israel."[18]

American Jewish organizations and Congress were justifiably suspicious of Ceausescu's true intentions. In June 1978, Senator Jackson wrote President Carter about Romania's "erratic emigration process," complaining that "Bucharest quickly processed emigration applications during congressional hearings but showed little interest in assisting emigrants during the remainder of the year."[19]

This indeed was Ceausescu's pattern. Whenever a high-ranking U.S. official from the State Department or Congress visited Romania, Ceausescu released a few dozen Jews and non-Jews who had waited years to emigrate. Whenever

Romania's Most Favored Nation status was due to be renewed, or when Romania came under the scrutiny of Congress, he accelerated emigration, later reducing it to its "normal" pace. While Congress repeatedly endorsed the MFN extension, it continued to express increasingly strong concerns about Romania's human rights situation.

In May 1983, Senator Jesse Helms met with the Romanian foreign minister, Stefan Andrei, and told him that "you have not lived up to the assurances and promises of last year."[20] Romania had not only failed to fulfill its emigration promises; in 1983 the U.S. Helsinki Watch Committee called Romania's human rights situation a disaster. Applicants for emigration became targets of discrimination; dissidents were routinely harassed and confined to psychiatric hospitals; typewriters had to be registered with the police; trade unions were prohibited or severely repressed; foreign contact was heavily restricted; publications were severely censored; and foreign journalists were constantly badgered.[21]

In October 1983 the Ceausescu regime claimed that the emigration purposefully encouraged by the West was becoming a "brain drain" for the nation. To compensate Romania, Ceausescu proposed a heavy tax "requiring would-be emigrants to reimburse the state for the cost of their education."[22] Although it was against the law in Romania to hold foreign currency, emigration candidates were asked to pay as much as $20,000 in hard cash in order to leave. Under West German, Israeli, and American pressure—including the threatened revocation of Romania's Most Favored Nation status—Ceausescu yielded, and the tax was not officially imposed.

Washington, outraged by Ceausescu's proposal, viewed it as further evidence of "Romania's inhumane practices."[23]

Bonn was equally upset by the treatment of ethnic Germans in Romania and made this clear to the Romanian government.

Yet Washington, Bonn, and Jerusalem also worried about Romania's anti-Semitic attitudes. A 1984 Library of Congress study reported, "There were repeated anti-Semitic outbursts in the official press and elsewhere that were condoned by the regime."[24] To forestall international reactions, in the 1960s the Romanian government had begun carefully camouflaging its anti-Semitism. Although it largely purged its administration of Jews, it maintained a few in high-ranking positions for decorative purposes, in order to demonstrate the quality of political power that Romanian Jews enjoyed.

After the Six-Day War, Romania did not, like the Soviet Union and the other Communist countries of Eastern Europe, launch a national anti-Zionist campaign. At least to international observers, for the next twenty years Romania seemed to support its small Jewish community. According to a Library of Congress report, "Romania's Jewish community in the late 1980s numbered between 20,000 and 25,000, of whom half were more than sixty-five years old. Jews enjoyed considerably more autonomy than any other religious denomination. . . . For twenty-five years the Jewish Federation in Romania had been allowed to publish a biweekly magazine in four languages. There were three ordained rabbis, and religious education was widely available to Jewish children. In addition, the government permitted the Jewish Federation to operate old-age homes and kosher restaurants."[25] As Ambassador Funderburk recalled, all this was possible because "Ceausescu made a deal with Israel to allow the Jews to emigrate to Israel in return for payments per head."[26]

Despite an official policy of tolerance, however, anti-Semitism was on the rise in the early 1980s. Anti-Semitic articles began to appear in heavily censored Romanian media. Between 1980 and 1985, according to Rabbi Rosen, "No one but Ceausescu was behind the savage campaign of hatred, of pogrom, incitement. Who would dare write in the journal of the Bucharest organization of the Communist Party *Saptamina* the article 'Ideals,' in which the court poet [Corneliu] Vadim [Tudor] used a language borrowed from Nazi literature, if he were not 'covered' by Ceausescu's Securitate."[27] In one of his many anti-Semitic articles, Tudor called the Jews "thieves and corrupters, people with no conscience and no sense of loyalty, who have no patriotic links whatsoever to their country and only think [of] how to exploit it."[28] Elena Ceausescu, who "had a definitive anti-Semitic streak and only a minimal understanding of the outside world," may also have been involved in this campaign.[29]

In May 1984, 190 members of the U.S. House of Representatives formed a congressional Human Rights Caucus and addressed a letter to Ceausescu indicating its "distress" over Romania's continued defiance of the Helsinki human rights provisions. The letter, according to Harrington and Courtney, "noted a number of anti-Semitic articles that had appeared in Romanian literature and the popular press, especially poems written by Corneliu Vadim Tudor. . . . The caucus also noted its concern about the 'direct and calculated persecution of fundamentalist Christians' and Bucharest's efforts to destroy the remnants of Hungarian culture in Romania."[30]

Ceausescu further damaged his relationship with Washington when he allowed his bureaucracy to recycle American Bibles into toilet paper. In June 1984 the *New York Times* and the *Wall Street Journal* reported that "Rolls of toilet paper contained fragments of biblical verses. The Romanian government permitted the World Reformed Alliance to ship 20,000 Bibles to the Reformed Church in Transylvania. The Alliance shipped the Bibles during the late 1970s and early 1980s. However, no one knows the number of Bibles that actually reached church congregations. The undistributed Bibles arrived at the paper and pulp [plants] at Braila and Bistrita, where they were recycled into toilet paper and first reappeared in state retail stores in February 1985."[31]

As Romania's reputation deteriorated, Ceausescu clung to a shred of credibility in the United States. Funderburk writes, "Romania was repeatedly thanked for attending the 1984 Summer Olympic games at Los Angeles. . . . On the other hand, America's position as the symbol of freedom, democracy, and human rights was eroded by its visits with Ceausescu, which appeared to most Romanians as support for his regime and policies."[32]

Another heavy blow was to follow. In May 1985 after resigning his diplomatic post in Romania, Ambassador Funderburk, in a long interview with the *Washington Post*, vehemently criticized Ceausescu and what he saw as Washington's "unduly friendly policy toward him."[33]

In December that year, Secretary of State George Shultz visited Bucharest and "warned [Ceausescu] that Romania could lose most-favored-nation status unless it changed its human rights policies. Both sides agreed to establish a system of consultation on human rights issues."[34] Ceausescu told Shultz that "no more Bibles are needed, and that freedom of religion was greater in Romania than in most other countries."[35] In a subsequent report to Washington, the American embassy characterized Romania as a "flashing yellow" situation.[36]

In February 1986, at Senate hearings on Romania's Most Favored Nation status, Assistant Secretary of State Rozanne Ridgeway's statement articulated the U.S. dilemma: "Our relations with Romania confront us with tough choices. On one side we have national security interests and our ability to positively affect the lives of individuals who need our support. On the other side we have a sense that our engagement brings us into association with a repressive regime that neither shares nor responds to the high principles of human rights that are so important to us."[37]

Again Washington warned Romania that its Most Favored Nation status would be repealed unless it improved its human rights record. Rosen was sent back to Washington to lobby, and on June 3 President Reagan granted a twelve-month extension. That same day he wrote Ceausescu to express strong concern over Romania's human rights issues, and closed, "Your government's unwillingness to accommodate these concerns has placed at risk our policy, which benefits Romania substantially."[38]

Ceausescu and his colleagues dismissed U.S. appeals. On August 29 and September 1, 1987, Representatives Steny Hoyer and Bill Richardson, Senator Frank Lautenberg, Assistant Secretary of State for Humanitarian Affairs Richard Schifter, and the staff director of the Helsinki Human Rights Commission, Ambassador Samuel Wise, traveled to Romania to meet with Ceausescu and Ioan Totu, his minister of foreign affairs. When the Americans raised the issue of human rights, Totu retorted that Romania was not obliged to respond to U.S. inquiries about human rights.

After all, Totu said, he had not chosen to mention such internal U.S. problems as the Iran-Contra affair.[39]

In 1987, against Senate opposition, Reagan once again extended Romania's Most Favored Nation status through July 1988.[40] In January that year, Deputy Secretary of State John Whitehead met in Bucharest with Ceausescu and presented him with another letter from Reagan, which again warned the Romanian president about his nation's human rights issues: "Without substantial improvements in the next three months, it will be very difficult for me to decide on renewed extension of MFN for Romania this spring, much less for the Congress to accept a positive recommendation."[41]

Ceausescu would not concede, and in a February letter told Reagan that Romania had decided to reject the requirements of Most Favored Nation status. "As regards democracy, we have created in Romania a unique broad-based democratic system . . . a system incomparably superior to many other democratic systems including that of the United States. . . . The laws of the country ensure equal rights and obligations: there is no discrimination or restriction of any kind. . . . We have decided to reject the extension of this clause under the conditions set forth by the Jackson-Vanik Amendment."[42]

According to Govrin, Romania hoped that after the November 1988 presidential election of George Bush, Washington's attitude toward Romania would improve. But America "showed no willingness to separate the human rights issue from granting MFN status to Romania, especially in light of the repressive acts undertaken by Romanian authorities toward Romanian dissidents."[43] Against all odds, Ceausescu hoped that his regime could somehow retain the role of maverick in American eyes.

Romanian relations with the United States now continued to deteriorate. In October 1988, Romanian authorities
protested the American embassy's contact with Romanian
dissidents.[44] Ceausescu nervously anticipated the Malta
Summit, as he was convinced that Washington and Moscow
were plotting against him.

In July 1989, Ambassador Kirk's posting in Romania
came to an end. The United States would not send another ambassador to Romania until after Ceausescu's dep-
osition. Govrin writes that in that month of Kirk's
departure, when President Bush visited Hungary and
Poland but not Romania, Romania's leadership was an-
gered, venting its irritation in articles and commentaries
"accusing President Bush of . . . striving to return to the
Cold War and . . . intending to undercut the stable socialist regimes of Eastern Europe by pushing them into anti-
socialist reforms of a capitalist nature."[45] According to
Kirk and Raceanu, Ceausescu "carefully noted U.S. White
House spokesman Marlon Fitzwater's statement shortly
after the Bush-Gorbachev summit in early December,
1989, that Bush had expressed concern to Gorbachev
about the situation in Romania."[46]

Romania's relations with its Western European partners
also worsened. France was outraged by the CIE's attempts
to kill Romanian dissidents living in Paris. In the mid-
1980s, West Germany's official criticism gave way to direct
acts of protest against Romanian policies. In April 1989
Chancellor Helmut Kohl declared that the "situation for
Romania's ethnic Germans had become intolerable."[47] And
the West German Foreign Ministry officially condemned
Romania's human rights policies. Israel, according to Govrin, also grew increasingly concerned about Romania's

human rights situation, aggravated by the rise in anti-Semitism and the demolition of synagogues.

Ultimately Ceausescu lost his prestige in the West because he could not (or would not) adapt to the spectacular changes occurring in the Soviet Union under Mikhail Gorbachev. The two men were arch enemies. Ceausescu hated Gorbachev for initiating *perestroika* and *glasnost*; Gorbachev despised Ceausescu for his Stalinism. On May 25, 1987, during a visit to Romania, Gorbachev had a heated session with Ceausescu. In his memoirs, Gorbachev recalls that the discussion became so loud that "one of the aides gave an order to close the windows, flung open on a warm night, and to move the guard further back into the park—no point in [having] witnesses."[48] Based on information from a Western colleague stationed in Bucharest, Govrin explains that Gorbachev's animus toward Ceausescu stemmed from three major sources: "Ceausescu's cult of personality that Gorbachev could not stand, with all of its implications for the way in which the state is led; Romania's inferior economic status, which connotes a negative model of the socialist-Communist regime in action; and Romania's blunt behavior at the Cultural Forum of the CSCE [Conference on Security and Cooperation in Europe] held in Bucharest several months earlier, which resulted in the failure to reach a unanimous, joint East-West resolution."[49]

Although Romania had erratically and only partially fulfilled Western desires for emigration, when it came to the question of human rights Ceausescu would not be moved. His regime's conduct at the CSCE conference reinforced Romania's sad reputation on the issue. A U.S. report summed up: "After a twenty-six-month review, an East-West consensus emerged, but Romania announced it was not bound by the agreement. From the start of negotiations, Romania had attempted to dilute the draft text prepared by the nonaligned states. During the final negotiations, it submitted seventeen amendments to remove human rights provisions from the final document. . . . Other delegations, including some from Warsaw Pact states, rejected these efforts. Romania's refusal to abide by the agreement drew universal condemnation from the other delegations and represented another step toward the international isolation of Ceausescu's Romania."[50]

U.S. support of the Ceausescu regime, and the granting of Most Favored Nation status, was, according to Kirk and Raceanu, "America's worst political and economic investment in the countries of Eastern Europe."[51] For support and trade failed to foster reform, and improved neither emigration to Israel nor Romania's human rights situation.

8

"Why Did You Drain My Soul?"

S ometimes I felt like saying to President Ceausescu: 'Why did you make it so hard for me over so many years? Why did you drain my soul?'"[1] Shaike Dan explained further: "True, it is just a drop, but it's from a faucet that drips all the time. . . . It must be emphasized that today more than 380,000 Romanian Jews live in Israel."[2] Prime Minister Shimon Peres held the same opinion. "I think that in terms of *alyah*, immigration to Israel, this is the largest, most exciting, least-known undertaking in the history of Israel, and [Dan] was the driving force behind this chapter."[3]

Leibovici-Lais, reflecting on Israeli-Romanian relations, has noted that because Romania was partially spared the human toll of the Holocaust, Romanian Jewry represented the most important source of emigrants for the new state of Israel.[4] Especially after the 1967 war, Israel considered Romania, in Israeli ambassador Abba Gefen's words, its "window on the Iron Curtain" and a potential "bridgehead for the renewal of relations with the countries of Eastern Europe."[5] Romania offered Israel "diplomatic respectability"[6] but also practical advantages—the unique opportunity to contact isolated Jewish communities in Communist Eastern Europe. In Govrin's words, "The communities were visited by members of the embassy staff and envoys of *Nativ*, who were an internal part of the embassy staff dealing with *alyah* matters and met local Jews daily who visited the embassy to receive information and guidance relating to their approach to Israel. . . . They also dealt with all matters involved in the immigration of the Jews from the USSR to Israel as they traveled through Romania."[7]

Israel in fact purchased Jews from countries other than Romania. In the late 1940s and early 1950s, Hungary was paid $1,000 per emigrant, and Bulgaria between $50 and $350.[8] Between 1956 and 1961, Israel bribed Moroccan authorities in order to smuggle its Jews to Israel through Spain on forged passports.[9] In 1971, Israel paid Saddam Hussein $1 million for the release of 1,246 Jews from Iraq.[10]

Between 1980 and 1985, Mossad, as a coordinator of Operation Moses, bribed Sudanese authorities in order to smuggle Falashas (Ethiopian Jews) out of Ethiopia, which reeled under famine and civil war.[11] In 1990 a crumbling Mengistu regime in Ethiopia received money from the Joint for the remaining twenty thousand Falashas to emigrate to Israel. Tens of millions of dollars were paid. According to Tad Szulc, Israel paid $2,427 per Falasha, "roughly what Ceausescu charged in Romania for an exit permit for a Jew."[12] There were others too, but no country sold Jews to Israel as avariciously and for such an extended period of time as Romania.

A high-ranking Israeli official recently remarked that the agreements with Romania "worked to the satisfaction of both sides."[13] This is only partly true. Israeli officials were always ill at ease over their deals with Romania. It boiled down, according to Jack Anderson and Dale Van Atta, to "buying slaves." But in so doing Israel was rescuing a community threatened by discrimination and economic and cultural extinction, at the same time strengthening Israel by infusing it with new immigrants. In short, "Israel secretly engaged in the longest and most expensive ransom arrangement in recent history."[14]

Israeli officials worried that the price paid by West Germany for ethnic Germans in Romania would be discovered by American authorities, who would then be curious about the emigration arrangements of Romanian Jews. Some Israeli leaders therefore lobbied for Romania's Most Favored Nation status, which temporarily buoyed Ceausescu's prestige and his treasury.[15]

But Israel was dealing with a regime and a dictator that were deeply involved with Arab terrorist organizations and with governments committed to Israel's destruction, and that cruelly oppressed their own population. As Raviv and Melman observe, in order to maintain the influx of Jewish immigrants, "Israel even appears to have neglected its own security concerns. Ceausescu had strong links with such enemies of Zionism as Libya's Muammar Gadhafi, Syria's Hafez al-Assad, and Yasser Arafat. Ceausescu trained their cadets [and] provided passports to Arab guerrillas."[16]

Israel accepted the risk. As Dan writes, "[I] warned Shimon Peres pending his expected meeting with the president of Romania, Nicolae Ceausescu. I described the character of the man, his rapacity, the repressive regime he'd imposed upon his countrymen, and his attempts to curry international recognition. I added that as long as such a meeting could get Jews out of there, it was worthwhile."[17] Leibovici-Lais recalls the Israeli government's resignation: "They referred with disgust to the slave trade. They were horrified, but they always reached the same conclusion: There is no other way out!"[18]

The granting of Most Favored Nation status, as Anderson and Van Atta wrote in a 1991 issue of the *Washington Post*, "was no small decision by the United States. Romanian dictator Nicolae Ceausescu was a brutal, almost psychopathic tyrant—qualities that the United States chose to ignore for decades. His people starved and froze to death because of his greedy ineptitude. . . . The truth about the ransoms and the effect they had on U.S. policy is a sensitive matter today. If Washington was pressured into a pro-Romanian policy to save the lives of some, what about the millions of others who died while the United States said nothing? If their pro-Romanian policy was based more on the fact that Ceausescu was seen as a maverick Communist, then the ransoms are only a fascinating footnote in history. But our information suggests that pro-Romanian Jewish advocates were influential in keeping Ceausescu on America's good side."[19]

The full story is more complex. Richard Nixon, seduced by Ceausescu, and in defiance of the State Department's opposition, endorsed the granting of Most Favored Nation status to Romania. Subsequent presidents, despite reservations, followed suit. Rosen and some American Jewish organizations endorsed the U.S. decision; other American Jewish organizations and circles in the Israeli government opposed it.

Officials in Washington probably had no hard evidence— until General Pacepa's defection—that Romania was selling Jews to Israel. Once they knew, they did nothing to upset the arrangement that allowed Jews and Germans to continue to emigrate. Ceausescu's maverick status also enabled him to maintain his slave trade. As Harrington and Courtney note, "During the first half of the 1980s, advocates of continuing Romanian MFN emphasized Romanian denunciation of the Soviet invasion of Czechoslovakia, criticism of Moscow's Afghanistan policy, obstructionism within the Warsaw Pact, and participation in the Los Angeles Summer Olympics, defying Moscow's boycott."[20]

Senator Henry Jackson and Representative Charles Vanik probably did not anticipate the extraordinary impact their amendment would have on American foreign policy. As Michael McFaul wrote, it was "a moral act . . . [and] one of the most successful foreign policy ideas initiated by Congress during the Cold War."[21] Gradually the Jackson-Vanik Amendment changed its focus from emigration to human rights. As Harrington and Courtney note, "Emigration remained a concern, but only one of many. . . . In 1974, the Jackson-Vanik criterion was emigration. In 1987, Jackson-Vanik meant human rights, religious freedom, and minority equality."[22] Ceausescu could not or would not keep pace.

Mikhail Gorbachev also contributed to Ceausescu's loss of support in Washington. "The new Soviet leader embraced many of Ceausescu's peace initiatives and in doing so ended Romania's 'maverick' identity. The argument that MFN rewarded Bucharest for its independence from Moscow was no longer valid. Stripped of this protection, Ceausescu's regime was laid bare for inspection, and its record of human rights violations forced even Romania's supporters to think twice about extending MFN, a privilege normally thought of as a reward for good behavior. . . . What remained was an ugly reality of human abuse and deprivation that even Moscow found distasteful. As Gorbachev moved toward détente, toward the twenty-first-century Europe, Washington's continued tolerance of Romania's behavior became a hindrance to future Soviet-American relations."[23]

Finally, Ceausescu's sale of sophisticated Soviet weaponry to the United States also proved to be a mistake. If Andropov or Gorbachev had found out about this trade, it would have placed Ceausescu in an extremely precarious position. Neither the Soviet leadership nor the KGB would have forgiven such an act by a member of the Warsaw Pact.

Ceausescu pretended to be evenhanded in his relations with Israel and the Arab states. Although in 1967 Romania maintained diplomatic relations with Israel, Ceausescu was decidedly pro-Arab. Quick to condemn "Israeli aggressions," he reluctantly condemned Arab terrorist acts. He never visited Israel, nor did he allow his prime ministers to do so, though he himself was officially invited. The leaders of Syria, Iraq, and Libya were "comrades," in ideology if not in arms. Commerce with Arab states was important to Ceausescu, but, as Melman and Raviv write, "like a bazaar trader, Ceausescu sold the Israelis secrets and information involving his Arab friends. He also had a role in the sensitive deal-making, including the groundwork, that led to the Israeli-Egyptian peace treaty and efforts to free Israeli prisoners and hostages held in Lebanon."[24]

Ceausescu mistrusted non-Romanians. Although his propaganda proclaimed equality between Romanians and ethnic minorities, his regime heavily discriminated against them, especially Hungarians and Jews. The ruler kept his anti-Semitism under wraps until the early 1980s. His regime prohibited anti-Zionist propaganda. He believed that the Jews had powerful international influence, and used

to say to his aide, Pacepa, "Romania has a proletariat dictatorship . . . America a Jewish dictatorship."[25]

When it came to the emigration of Jews, Germans, and
the few thousand Romanians who were allowed to leave the
country, Ceausescu was a hypocrite. On one hand he negotiated emigration directly with Dan and Huesch; on the
other hand he repeatedly condemned those who sought to
emigrate. Beginning in the late 1970s, according to a Library of Congress study, Ceausescu launched a duplicitous
media campaign. "Spokespersons for ethnic minorities in
the workers' councils praised the regime's treatment of minorities and declared their devotion to socialist Romania.
By contrast, those who desired to emigrate were depicted as
weaklings with underdeveloped 'patriotic and political con-
sciousness,' would-be traitors abandoning their fatherland
and the struggle to build socialism. Stories abounded [in the
Romanian media] of Romanians emigrating only to find life
more difficult in their new environment and happily returning to their homeland. . . . Obtaining permission to
leave the country was a lengthy, expensive, and exhausting
process. Prospective emigrants were likely to be fired from
their jobs or demoted to positions of lower prestige and pay.
They were often evicted from their homes and publicly cas-
tigated. At the same time, they were denied medical care
and other social benefits, and their children were not permitted to enroll in schools."[26] By comparison, Ceausescu's
code of honor made that of a second-rate mobster sparkle.

Pacepa vividly describes the Romanian dictator. He was
"constantly in a state of agitation, contorting his face in an
effort to overcome his stutter and spattering saliva all
around when he spoke. . . . [He] had belonged to what Marx
called the Lumpenproletariat—a shoemaker's apprentice

who never practiced his humble craft but instead earned his living by craftiness. . . . [He] could hardly read or write, [he] was a sick megalomaniac, who paid lip service to Marxism only to achieve his own ends. Ceausescu's reign covered twenty-four years and turned Gheorghiu-Dej's Romania upside-down and inside-out. . . . In 1966 he replaced Romania's military high command with his own men, allegedly to move out aging Stalinist holdovers. Once in the saddle, Ceausescu also moved to create his own brand of Marxism, called Ceausism—a ludicrous mixture of Marxism, Leninism, Stalinism, nationalism, Roman arrogance, and Byzantine fawning that was so slippery, undefined, and ever-changing that he filled thirty-four volumes of his collected works without being able to describe it."[27]

The head of Ceausescu's chancellery, Silviu Curticeanu, who knew him perhaps better than any of his colleagues, thought the dictator's dominant characteristic was "shrewdness. . . . A diabolical one . . . quick and cunning in all circumstances, he was often perfidious, two-faced, and hypocritical. . . . Another feature of his character was toughness. Severe and austere, totally lacking humor, Ceausescu used toughness as a tool to impose his points of view every time his shrewdness and arguments were not sufficient."[28]

Curticeanu calls Elena Ceausescu, who beginning in the early 1970s was second in command in the Romanian Communist hierarchy, Ceausescu's "major weakness. . . . She does not deserve to be characterized. In order to do it, an inventory of all the negative human features known to history is sufficient; dominant were meanness and avarice, stupidity, and crass lack of culture."[29]

Ion Gheorghe Maurer and Emil Bodnaras, both members of the Politburo, bear the heavy historical burden of having empowered Ceausescu in 1965. In 1972, Bodnaras multiplied his guilt: he proposed that Elena Ceausescu be made a member of the Romanian Communist party's Politburo.[30]

Gradually Romania's government began to function according to the whims of the Ceausescus. Govrin describes an April 1986 parliamentary session: "Aside from the Ceausescu couple, mentioned at least six times by each of the speakers, no other name was mentioned, not the government members nor those of the Politburo members. The listener was supposed to reach only one conclusion: before Ceausescu's rise to power, Romania had never known economic or democratic progress (this is why Ceausescu's twenty-year rule was called the 'golden era'), and until Elena Ceausescu's nomination as head of the National Council for Scientific Research (with status equivalent to a minister), Romania had never known scientific progress . . ."[31] An aide to Rabbi Rosen, professor Alexandru Vianu, described Ceausescu to Govrin in 1987 as being "unbalanced [and] close to madness."[32]

Although Romania was more independent of Moscow than other Soviet-bloc nations, Western intelligence officials never assumed that the Ceausescu regime betrayed its Soviet allies out of a secret affection for U.S. policy or Western ideology. As Benjamin Weiser noted in the *Washington Post*, "It was just greed—pure and simple personal greed."[33] Alexandru Barladeanu, a former Politburo member who opposed Ceausescu, declared that "Ceausescu sold Germans and Jews as slaves through Securitate, and the funds obtained were morally tainted."[34] When it came to profiting from emigration, morality was Ceausescu's least concern. The Romanian Communist government succeeded where its fascist predecessors had failed: it not only eliminated Romanian Jews, it profited from them.[35]

A young Romanian historian, Marius Oprea, recently reflected, "The trade with human beings practiced by the Bucharest authorities is a page of the history of communism closely guarded from curious eyes."[36] It is also a page that Israeli authorities are reluctant to reveal. Yet sooner or later historical truth comes to light. In May 1987 the Romanian minister of foreign affairs, Adrian Severin, officially apologized on behalf of the Romanian government for "deporting tens of thousands of ethnic Germans to labor camps during Communist rule or selling them by demanding cash from the Bonn government for emigration permits." He referred to "dishonorable bargains claiming substantial financial compensation for reunifying ethnic German families from Romania who wanted to settle in Germany."[37] Severin declared at a news conference with his German counterpart, Klaus Kinkel, "We express deep regret and apologize for what happened. . . . This is a gesture of moral reparation for Romanian citizens and German citizens of Romania—whose destinies remain definitely marked by such lamentable actions."[38]

The Romanian government has not similarly apologized to the government of Israel nor to the Romanian Jews it oppressed and sold.

Afterword

ON THE WARM, sunny day of July 22, 1978, I was walking with Romanian president Nicolae Ceausescu along the restricted presidential shore of Lake Techirghiol, waiting for the mud covering our naked bodies to crack. This was the most famous of the Romanian lakes believed to have miraculous therapeutic qualities for arthritis, sexual impotence, and infertility. For best results, its mud routine prescribed that the patient undergo treatment in several stages. First you took a naked bath in the lake, which was so salty you could read a newspaper as you floated around. Next you covered yourself with mud and stood in the sun to dry, with raised arms and parted legs, letting a hard crust form. Then you walked around until your shell began to crack. Finally you took another bath in the lake and washed the mud off.

Old-fashioned in matters of health, Ceausescu was as loyal to Lake Techirghiol as he was to his personal political goals. For more than twenty years he had gone there every July for the mudpack treatment. In the early days he had hoped the mud would keep him from getting arthritis; now he hoped it would cure it.

"How much last month from the *jidani*?" Ceausescu asked me, rubbing thumb and forefinger together to make it clear he was talking money. In Romanian the word *jidan* is the most derogatory epithet for a Jew.

"One hundred twenty-two thousand," I answered. "Dollars in cash."

Ceausescu swung his head out like a snake. "Is that all?" A dry clump fell from his Adam's apple and sank into the sand.

Six days after that last walk with Ceausescu on the Techirghiol beach, I was magnanimously granted political asylum by the United States government, in spite of my position as one of the leaders of the Soviet-bloc intelligence community. Diplomatic reports from Romania later recounted that Ceausescu had ripped his shirt into shreds when he heard I had defected, and then had abruptly disappeared from public view. He closeted himself with his wife at their summer residence on the Black Sea and surrounded the place with a cordon of armored vehicles and security troops. Before the day was over, armored personnel carriers of the security police began patrolling the streets of Bucharest as well.

All Soviet-bloc rulers would have trembled in their boots at the news that their spy chief had defected to the United States. (No others did so either before or after me.) Ceausescu had an additional reason, for I was among the handful of his closest advisers who knew he was living a life of extravagant luxury made possible by money obtained from trading in human beings.

Just one month before I broke with him, Ceausescu had ordered my espionage service to fatten his personal bank account with one *billion* in cash dollars extorted from the

West. Of course, my service was not able to meet that ridiculous amount. Nevertheless, on July 24, 1978, when I left Romania for good, Ceausescu's personal account held a balance of some $400 million—though his wife, Elena, had made a substantial dent in it by buying French furs and jewelry for herself. A substantial portion of this $400 million came from Ceausescu's trade in human beings.

The ransom of the Jews was one of the most despicable by-products of communism. This feudal practice entailed three evils. The first was the Communist rulers' belief that they owned their people and held the right of life and death over them. Some 100 million human beings perished at the hands of their regimes in the Soviet Union, Eastern Europe, and Red China. Millions more are still living as slaves in North Korea.

The second evil was the Kremlin's anti-Semitism, which epitomized the organic connection between communism and Nazism. The general perception is that Germany was the cradle of contemporary anti-Semitism. It was not. Before we had the word *holocaust* we had the word *pogrom*, meaning massacre. To the ancient Greeks, a holocaust was simply a burnt sacrifice, and it was not until the 1930s that the Nazis invented the Jewish Holocaust. Russia's first major pogrom against the Jews took place on April 15, 1881, in the Ukrainian town of Yelisavetgrad, named for the Empress Elizabeth.

Tsarist anti-Semitism persisted beyond tsarist Russia. When Stalin decided to dispose of his chief rival, Leon Trotsky (né Lev Davidovich Bronstein), he portrayed him as a Jewish spy in the service of Zionism and expelled him from the country. The insinuation also allowed Stalin to arrange for Trotsky's murder in Mexico City without causing so much as a blink from most of the world. The first chairman of the Comintern, Grigory Zinoviev (né Ovsel Gershon Aronov Radomyslsky), who was also born into a bourgeois Jewish family, was later sentenced to death for organizing a "terrorist center" for the assassination of government and Communist party leaders, financed by Zionism; he was shot on August 21, 1936.

After World War II the Kremlin's anti-Semitism was rapidly embraced by the political police services created by Moscow in Eastern Europe. The Romanian Securitate was one of them. After I broke with communism, Ceausescu did not use his propaganda or party machinery to compromise me—not a single article about me appeared in Romania. Instead Ceausescu ordered the Securitate to spread the rumor within the country that I was a *jidan* traitor (though I am not a Jew), and that I had left Romania illegally with help from American Zionist espionage organizations when I learned that the Securitate was ready to arrest me for trafficking in drugs and whiskey. It worked. After Ceausescu's death, in June 1999 Romania's Supreme Court canceled the two death sentences ordered for me by Ceausescu and decreed that my military rank and properties be returned to me. Nevertheless the Romanian government refused, and still refuses, to carry out that Court decision, and no politician in that country has protested. Evidently, quite a few people in the current Romanian government and in political parties there still hate the *jidani*.

The third evil of communism was the regularity with which its political triumph produced economic ruin. Whether in transforming Russia from the world's greatest agricultural exporter before the 1917 revolution—when it supplied one-quarter of Europe's wheat—into the world's

greatest grain importer, or in transforming oil-rich Romania into Europe's Ethiopia, communism invariably destroyed the national economy wherever it came to power.
Without private ownership, competition, and individual in-
centive, Communist governments proved incapable of producing economic progress and therefore real, convertible
money.

In the Soviet bloc, money lost its economic regulatory
function. It became merely an instrument for expressing
domestic wages and prices. Like the Soviet ruble, the Romanian *leu* and the other Communist national currencies
also became nonconvertible—that is, they had value only
within their own countries and could not be used as a
medium of exchange in international trade.

Instead of real money that could circulate from country
to country, the Soviet Union began using bureaucratic
monetary units in its export-import operations. In Romania
that monetary unit was called the *leu-valuta* (LV). Its value
was different for each item being traded on the international market and was established by the *leu*-to-the-dollar
price of a given exported or imported product. Bucharest
considered an export or import profitable if its LV value was
close to the legal exchange rate, which during my last year
in Communist Romania was 15 *lei* to the dollar. In that
same 1978 year, however, the LV for exporting a dozen eggs
was 102, and for importing a color television set 2,000.

Irrational, unpredictable, and chaotic, this monetary
scheme brought dissipation and debauchery to the Communist bloc's foreign trade—and a chronic lack of real, Western
money to its treasuries. Without having real money at hand,
Romania, like the rest of the former Soviet-bloc countries,
based most of its foreign trade on barter operations: machine

tools for oil, raw materials for lumber, and so forth. In the early years of communism, Moscow and Bucharest had few needs for real Western money; among the foremost were payments for espionage, for the importation of prohibited equipment for the military industry, and for the purchase of consumer goods for leading bureaucrats. At that time, Moscow—and Bucharest—obtained those cash dollars mostly by selling gold on the Western market.

The Soviet bloc's incapacity to generate real money on its own eventually compelled the Kremlin to transform the Soviet-bloc espionage community into a huge mechanism for producing Western currency. In 1954, Khrushchev charged the espionage service to produce a significant part of the cash dollars needed by the Soviet government. He began by extorting money from emigrés living in the West. Soon his "inheritance operations"—the name given to the procedure of fleecing the emigrés—expanded throughout the Soviet bloc and grew into a refined art form, as Radu Ioanid describes in this book. Over the years I spent in Romania, many things changed in the bloc intelligence community, but its inheritance operations continued to be run just as they had been originally conceived. "We cannot nationalize their assets in the West, but we'll make them pay for it," remained Moscow's broken record until my very last day under communism.

In the mid-1950s the Kremlin laid the foundation for a new espionage specialty: "scam operations" for acquiring hard currency from the Soviet Union's import-export projects with Western firms. The Romanian espionage service followed step, and over the next years it refined its scam operations to the point where they became one of Romania's major producers of hard currency. Bucharest's contract with

Atomic Energy of Canada Limited (AECL) for its uranium reactors, which I was charged with overseeing, is a telling example. Almost every Romanian involved in that contract—several hundred in all—was an undercover officer or agent in charge of deceiving the Canadians and stealing from them. As a Canadian journalist later wrote, "Once called the salvation of the nuclear industry, Canada's export of nuclear reactors to Romania has become a disaster involving misappropriated funds, the dumping of Romanian goods in Canada, and the giveaway of advanced technology paid for by Canadian taxpayers. . . ."

In the late 1950s, Romania's search for Western currency received an unexpected shot in the arm. The Israeli foreign intelligence service, Mossad, which was also responsible for extricating Jews from countries that did not have free emigration, passed the word that Tel Aviv was prepared to pay Bucharest secret cash dollars for each Jew who would be allowed to emigrate. In order to preserve the secrecy of the operation, the Israelis insisted that its management be confined to the foreign intelligence services of the two countries.

Romania's sale of its people as an export commodity was approved by Nikita Khrushchev in October 1958, during the Soviet premier's six-day vacation in Bucharest. I was present at the discussions. Initially Khrushchev reacted in a tirade against the "swindler *zhidi* usurers" who, he raged, believed they could buy the Communists as they had bought America. During dinner, however, Khrushchev changed his mind. He insisted that Romania take products, not cash, from the *zhidi*, so that even if news of the emigration operation eventually leaked, it would not appear to be a naked sale of slaves. Khrushchev's choice of a barter object was livestock farms; he considered himself an agricultural expert.

In the ensuing six years, various Western firms were secretly paid with Tel Aviv's money to build modern farms for pigs, cattle, sheep, chickens, and turkeys in Romania. Most of the farms were located in or around the town of Periș, some thirty miles north of Bucharest. For reasons of secrecy, all these assets were managed by the Securitate, which thereupon became the largest ham, beef, lamb, poultry, and egg exporter in Romania. The money obtained from that hideous barter—between $8 million and $10 million a year by the mid-1960s—was deposited into a secret bank account that only Gheorghe Gheorghiu-Dej, the Romanian dictator at the time, could access. No other member of the Romanian government knew of this odious trade, and even within my espionage service only a handful of officers were familiar with the Israelis' involvement in the Periș farms.

After Gheorghiu-Dej's death, Ceausescu, his successor, established per-head prices for the Jews who were allowed to emigrate—depending on education, profession, and employment—and demanded that the Mossad pay in hard cash. When Tel Aviv agreed, Ceausescu ordered the espionage service to initiate a similar cash operation with West Germany, which was already "buying" Germans from East Germany. In the four years before my defection, the espionage service worked around the clock to sell off Romanian Jews, Romanian Germans, and Romanian Romanians while pocketing substantial amounts of cash dollars. All those proceeds were deposited in special bank accounts that could be used only by Ceausescu.

Despite my report to the United States government—following my defection—about this human trade, and despite journalists' investigations that confirmed it, Romania's sale of Jews became a kind of open secret: everyone was aware of it, but no one wanted to acknowledge it officially. This book will finally change that curious situation.

The roots of *The Ransom of the Jews* go back to 1993, when the United States Holocaust Memorial Museum opened. A few weeks later, when I visited it, I learned that the historian responsible for the museum's outstanding photographic displays was not a Holocaust survivor but a young Romanian immigrant.

So was born my friendship with Radu Ioanid, and the idea of publishing this book. For years I described to Radu the super-secret documents on the ransom of the Jews, and where they could be found in the still-classified archives of the Romanian espionage service. And for years Radu lobbied members of Congress and leaders of international Jewish organizations to help him pry those papers out of Romania. Eventually the government in Bucharest succumbed—though there are many more incriminating documents about this hideous sale of Jews still buried in the archives.

Unfortunately the Israeli government continues to believe that it is still bound by the secrecy agreement it signed with Ceausescu's espionage service. But Radu Ioanid persevered. Eventually he obtained comprehensive testimony from Shlomo Leibovici-Lais, a heroic Israeli figure who spent most of his life helping the Israeli government save Jews from Romania under both the Nazi and the Communist dictatorships.

After World War II ended, some of the Nazi concentration camps were transformed into museums of freedom, offering the world confirmation that the awful past would never be repeated. The Communist ransom of the Jews is another crime of historic proportions. I hope this book will prevent that aberration from ever recurring.

ION MIHAI PACEPA
Lieutenant General (ret.)

Appendix

Emigration from Romania to Israel, 1948–1989*

Year	Number of emigrants
May 15, 1948–1949	31,274
1950	47,071
1951	40,625
1952	3,712
1953	61
1954	53
1955	235
1956	714
1957	594
1958	8,954
1959	8,360
1960	9,321
1961	21,269
1962	9,878
1963	13,243
1964	25,926
1965	10,949
1966	3,467

*Sources: Shlomo Leibovici-Lais / ACMEOR Archives, and Yosef Govrin, *Israeli-Romanian Relations at the End of the Ceausescu Era*, p. 261.

Year	Number of emigrants
1967	779
1968	226
1969	1,754
1970	5,614
1971	1,861
1972	3,005
1973	4,123
1974	3,729
1975	2,393
1976	2,223
1977	1,501
1978	1,223
1979	1,113
1980	1,241
1981	1,179
1982	1,720
1983	1,340
1984	2,010
1985	1,374
1986	1,348
1987	1,673
1988	1,473
1989	1,499

Notes

INTRODUCTION: LOST AND FOUND

1. Ion Mihai Pacepa, *Red Horizons: Chronicles of a Communist Spy Chief* (Washington, D.C., 1987), p. 76.

2. Mihai Pelin, *Din culisele spionajului romanesc, DIE 1955–1980* (Bucharest, 1997), p. 250.

3. Ibid., pp. 306, 398.

4. Ibid., p. 399.

5. Ibid., p. 387.

6. Interview with Cornel Burtica, Bucharest, March 23, 2002.

7. Amos Ettinger, *Blind Jump: The Story of Shaike Dan* (New York, 1992), p. 14.

1. "THE JEWS ARE OUR MISFORTUNE"

1. Carol Iancu, *Les Juifs de Roumanie, 1866–1919: De L'Exclusion a l'Emancipation* (Aix en Provence, 1978), pp. 186–187.

2. Carol Iancu, *Bleichröder et Crémiaux, Le combat pour l'émancipation des Juifs de Roumanie devant le Congres de Berlin, Correspondence inédite (1878–1880)* (Montpellier, 1987), p. 29.

3. Carol Iancu, *L'émancipation des Juifs de la Roumanie* (Montpellier, 1992), p. 32.

4. Israel Bar-Avi, *O istorie a Evreilor Romani, Emigrarile anului 1900* (Jerusalem, 1961), p. 150; quote from *Die Welt*, June 15, 1900.

5. Gheorghe Dumitras-Bitoaica, *Statutul juridic al evreilor si legislatia romanizarii* (Bucharest, 1942), p. 121.

6. Beate Klarsfeld Foundation, *Documents Concerning the Fate of Romanian Jewry During the Holocaust* [hereafter *DCFJRJDH*] (New York, 1988), vol. 3, p. 310.

7. Aurica Simion, *Preliminarii politico-diplomatice ale insurectiei romane din august 1944* (Cluj, 1979), p. 125.

8. United States Holocaust Memorial Museum/Romanian Information Service [hereafter USHMM/SRI], RG 25.004M, roll 32, fond 40010, vol. 1r.

9. United States Holocaust Memorial Museum/Romanian State Archives [hereafter USHMM/RSA], RG 25.002M, roll 18, fond Presedentia Consiliului de Ministrii, cabinet, Dosar 167/1941.

10. USHMM/SRI, RG 25.004M, fond 40010, vol. 78.

11. USHMM/SRI, RG 25.004M, roll 31, fond 40010, vol. 1.

12. Tuvia Friling, *Arrow in the Dark: David Ben-Gurion, the Yishuv Leadership, and Rescue Attempts During the Holocaust* (Madison, Wisc., 2004).

13. *New York Times*, February 16, 1943. The ad and its implications and consequences are analyzed at length by David Wyman in *The Abandonment of the Jews: America and the Holocaust, 1941–1946* (New York, 1984), pp. 85–87.

14. *New York Times*, February 13, 1943, C.L. Sulzberger, "Romania Proposes Transfer of Jews."

15. Tuvia Friling, *Arrow in the Dark*, chapter 5.

16. Mihail Sebastian, *Journal, 1935–1944* (Chicago, 2000), p. 408.

17. NARA, RG 84, US Embassy Ankara, General records, 1941, file 840.1, Situation of the Jews in Romania.

18. Ira Hirschmann, *Life Line to a Promised Land* (New York, 1946), p. 26.

19. Ibid., p. 46.

20. Ibid., p. 49.

21. Ibid.

22. NARA, RG 84, US Embassy Ankara, General records, 1941, file 840.1, Situation of the Jews in Romania.

23. Hirschmann, *Life Line*, p. 52.

24. Ibid., p. 54.

25. Ira Hirschmann, *Caution to the Winds* (New York, 1962), p. 156.

26. Ibid., p. 157.

27. Dalia Ofer, *Escaping the Holocaust: Illegal Immigration to the Land of Israel, 1939–1944* (New York, 1990), appendixes.

28. Amos Ettinger, *Blind Jump: The Story of Shaike Dan* (New York, 1992), p. 47.

29. Ibid., p. 43.

30. Hirschmann, *Life Line*, pp. 78–79.

31. Yitzhak (Menu) Ben-Efraim, *From Land Under Siege to People Besieged: The Israeli Parachutists in Romania in World War II. A Personal Testimony*, in Studia Judaica X (Cluj-Napoca 2001), p. 100.

32. *Cartea alba a securitatii* (Bucharest, 1996), vol. II, p. 406.

33. Itzhak Artzi, *Biografia unui sionist* (Bucharest, 1999), p. 115; Yitzhak (Menu) Ben-Efraim, *From Land Under Siege*, p. 104.

2. VOTING WITH THEIR FEET

1. Winston S. Churchill, *The Second World War, Triumph and Tragedy*, vol. VI (Boston, 1985), pp. 198–199.

2. American Jewish Archives/World Jewish Congress Report [hereafter AJA/WJCR], OSS/Romania, June 9, 1945, p. 2.

3. *DCFRJDH*, vol. 6, p. 606.

4. Moses Rosen, *Dangers, Tests and Miracles: The Remarkable Life Story of Chief Rabbi Rosen of Romania as told by Joseph Finklestone* (London, 1990), p. 49.

5. Liviu Rotman, "Romanian Jewry, The First Decade After the Holocaust," in Randolph Braham, *The Tragedy of Romanian Jewry* (New York, 1994), p. 291.

6. Ettinger, *Blind Jump*, pp. 115–116.

7. USHMM/SRI, RG 25.004M, file 4720, concerning Rabbi Zissu Portugal.

8. Andrei Roth, *Who 'Brought' Communism to Romania and Who 'Destroyed' It*, Radio Free Europe, EEP Report, December 7, 2000, Volume 2, number 22.

9. *Daily Intelligence Summary*, April 27, 1945, A 17/8A, UJA, American Jewish Archives.

10. Ettinger, *Blind Jump*, p. 158.

11. Rotman, "Romanian Jewry," p. 300.

12. Abba Gefen, *Israel at a Crossroads* (Jerusalem, 2001), p. 186.

13. Rotman, "Romanian Jewry," p. 302.

14. Ettinger, *Blind Jump*, pp. 124, 157.

15. Ehud Avriel, *Open the Gates! A Personal Story of "Illegal" Immigration to Israel* (New York, 1975), pp. 192–193.

16. Ettinger, *Blind Jump*, pp. 120, 157–158.

17. Interview with Shlomo Leibovici-Lais, May 11, 2001.

18. Dennis Deletant, *Ceausescu and the Securitate: Coercion and Dissent in Romania, 1965–1989* (London, 1995), pp. 4, 15.

19. Vladimir Tismaneanu, *Fantoma lui Gheorghiu-Dej* (Bucharest, 1995), p. 204.

20. Ettinger, *Blind Jump*, pp. 121–122, 158.

21. Ibid., p. 161.

22. Ibid., pp. 161–162.

23. USHMM/SRI, RG 25.004M, folder 4005, vol. 160, pp. 121–140, Interrogation of Melania Iancu.

24. Ettinger, *Blind Jump*, p. 166.

25. Ibid., pp. 171, 185–186.

26. Itzhak Artzi, *Biografia unui sionist* (Bucharest, 1999), pp. 146, 148.

27. Ettinger, *Blind Jump*, pp. 161, 176–177.

28. Ibid., p. 208.

29. Ibid., pp. 208–209.

30. Interview with Shlomo Leibovici-Lais, May 11, 2001.

31. USHMM/SRI, RG 25.004M, folder 40009, vol. 14, pp. 259–260, Interrogation of Alexandru Jurim.

32. Ettinger, *Blind Jump*, p. 206.

33. Romanian State Archives /Arhiva Comitetului Central al Partidului Comunist Roman (hereafter RSA/CCRCP), code I–106, CDE report, December 28, 1950, p. 319.

3. THE ZIONIST ENEMY

1. *Romania-Israel, Ministerul Afacerilor Externe, documente diplomatice, vol. I*, 1948–1969 (Bucharest, 2000), pp. 6–10.

2. Joshua Rubenstein and Vladimire P. Naumov, eds., *Stalin's Secret Pogrom: The Postwar Inquisition of the Jewish Anti-Fascist Committee* (New Haven, 2001), p. 40.

3. Ettinger, *Blind Jump*, pp. 263–276, 290–296.

4. Rubenstein and Naumov, *Stalin's Secret Pogrom*, p. 41.

5. Ibid., p. 46.

6. Ibid., p. 50.

7. Ibid., p. 60.

8. RSA/CCRCP, code I–106, CDE report, December 28, 1950, p. 319; Rotman, "Romanian Jewry," p. 315.

9. Interview with Shlomo Leibovici-Lais, Tel Aviv, May 11, 2001.

10. Robert Levy, *Ana Pauker: The Rise and Fall of a Jewish Communist* (Berkeley, 2001), p. 167.

11. Rotman, "Romanian Jewry," p. 312.

12. Rosen, *Dangers*, p. 50.

13. RSA/CCRCP, Department of Foreign Affairs, folder 14, 1945.

14. Alexandre Safran, *Resisting the Storm: Romania, 1940–1947: Memoirs* (Jerusalem, 1987), p. 191.

15. Ibid., pp. 194, 202.

16. Ibid.

17. Ibid., p. 289.

18. Rosen, *Dangers*, p. 60.

19. USHMM/SRI, folder 28827, vol. 1.

20. Rosen, *Dangers*, p. 63.

21. USHMM/SRI, RG 25. 004M, roll 148, file 7623, vol. 3.

22. Interrogation of Melania Iancu, SRI Archives, fond Y, folder 40005, vol. 160, pp. 121–140. See also Levy, *Ana Pauker*, pp. 213–220.

23. Levy, *Ana Pauker*, p. 171.

24. Ibid.

25. Interview with Shlomo Leibovici-Lais, Tel Aviv, May 5, 2001.

26. Florian Banu, "Foametea din '46 si cresterea antisemitismului in Moldova," in *Romania: A Crossroads of Europe* (Iasi, 2002), p. 246.

27. Levy, *Ana Pauker*, pp. 165–166.

28. Deletant, *Ceausescu and the Securitate*, p. 63.

29. Archive of CCRCP, codul I, 106, fond 37, Comitetul Democratic Evreiesc, CDE Report, March 3, 1946.

30. Ibid., CDE Report, December 28, 1950.

31. Banu, "Foametea din '46 si cresterea antisemitismului in Moldova," pp. 254–255, 257.

32. Safran, *Resisting the Storm*, p. 242.

33. Ibid., p. 228.

34. Ibid., pp. 232, 274.

35. Levy, *Ana Pauker*, pp. 166, 332.

36. Mihai Pelin, *Sionisti sub ancheta, AL Zissu, declaratii, confruntari, interogatorii, 10 mai 1951–1 martie 1952* (Bucharest, 1993), p. 256.

37. Ibid., p. 263.

38. *Romania-Israel, documente diplomatice*, vol. 1, p. 73.

39. Rubenstein and Naumov, *Stalin's Secret Pogrom*, p. 61.

40. *Romania-Israel, documente diplomatice*, vol. 1, p. 103.

41. Dan Raviv and Yossi Melman, *Every Spy a Prince: The Complete History of Israel's Intelligence Community* (Boston, 1989), p. 18.

42. Ian Black and Benny Morris, *Israel's Secret Wars: A History of Israel's Intelligence Services* (New York, 1991), pp. 79–80.

43. Ibid., p. 80.

44. Ibid., pp. 81, 82.

45. Ibid., p. 83; Raviv and Melman, *Every Spy a Prince*, pp. 29–30.

46. Black and Morris, *Israel's Secret Wars*, p. 551.

47. Ibid.

48. Ibid., p. 552.

49. Mihai Pelin, *Sionisti sub ancheta*, p. 46.

50. Archives of CCRCP, Chancellery, folder 24, 1949.

51. Levy, *Ana Pauker*, p. 173.

52. *Romania-Israel, documente diplomatice*, vol. 1, p. 26.

53. Ibid., p. 32.

54. Levy, *Ana Pauker*, p. 183.

55. Rosen, *Dangers*, p. 82.

56. Levy, *Ana Pauker*, p. 188.

57. Ibid., pp. 188–189.

58. Ibid., pp. 189, 192.

59. Rosen, *Dangers*, p. 83.

60. Ibid., p. 91.

61. Ibid., pp. 84, 87.

62. Levy, *Ana Pauker*, p. 172.

63. Ibid., p. 173.

64. SRI Archives, Folder 10090, p. 324.

65. Archive of CCRCP, codul I, 106, fond 37, Comitetul Demo-cratic Evreiesc, Report of CDE on December 28, 1950.

66. Levy, *Ana Pauker*, p. 176.

67. Archive of CCRCP, codul I, 106, fond 37, Comitetul Demo-cratic Evreiesc, Report of CDE, December 28, 1950.

68. Interview with Shlomo Leibovici-Lais, Tel Aviv, May, 11, 2001.

69. Andrew and Leslie Cockburn, *The Inside Story of U.S.-Israeli Covert Relations* (Toronto, 1991), p. 22.

70. Ibid., p. 23.

71. Romanian Foreign Ministry Archives, fond Israel, 1945–1949, pp. 211–224.

72. Interview with Shlomo Leibovici-Lais, Tel Aviv, May, 11, 2001.

73. SRI Archives, folder 10090, pp. 403–404.

74. Yossi Melman and Dan Raviv, "Buying Romania's Jews: How Israel Ransomed 120,000 People from Ceausescu," *Washington Post*, January 14, 1990.

75. Romanian Foreign Ministry Archives, fond Israel, 1945–1949, pp. 211–224.

76. Ettinger, *Blind Jump*, pp. 305–306.

77. Joseph F. Harrington and Bruce J. Courtney, *Tweaking the Nose of the Russians* (New York, 1991), p. 18.

78. Philippe Marguerat, *Le IIIeme Reich et le petrole roumain* (Geneva, 1977), p. 206.

79. Harrington and Courtney, *Tweaking the Nose of the Russians*, p. 19.

80. Ibid., pp. 20–21.

81. Ibid., p. 28.

82. Ibid., pp. 105–106.

83. Ettinger, *Blind Jump*, pp. 322–323.

84. Interview with Shlomo Leibovici-Lais, Tel Aviv, May 5, 2001; letter to the author from Shlomo Leibovici-Lais; phone conversation with Shlomo Leibovici-Lais, October 5, 2002.

85. Ephraim Illin, *Al Hechatum*, pp. 198–199.

86. Ibid.

87. Ibid., pp. 191–192.
88. Ettinger, *Blind Jump*, p. 323.

4. BARTER

1. Harrington and Courtney, *Tweaking the Nose of the Russians*, p. 107.
2. Ibid., p. 114.
3. Ibid., pp. 116–117.
4. Ibid., pp. 118–119.
5. Ibid., p. 146.
6. Ibid., p. 144.
7. Rosen, *Dangers*, p. 115.
8. Raviv and Melman, *Every Spy a Prince*, pp. 38, 40; Interview with Shlomo Leibovici-Lais, Tel Aviv, May 11, 2001.
9. Interview with Shlomo Leibovici-Lais, Tel Aviv, May 11, 2001.
10. Harrington and Courtney, *Tweaking the Nose of the Russians*, p. 141.
11. Ibid., pp. 142–143.
12. Ibid., p. 149.
13. Ibid., p. 166.
14. Ibid., p. 169.
15. Rosen, *Dangers*, p. 152.
16. Ibid., p. 153.
17. *Romania-Israel, Documente diplomatice, 1948–1969*, pp. 117–118.
18. Ibid., pp. 114–117.
19. Ibid., pp. 127, 139.
20. Ibid., p. 146.
21. *Cartea alba a securitatii*, vol. III, 1994, Report of the U.S. embassy in Bucharest dated February 26, 1964, titled "Evreii din Romania: o minoritate descrescinda" (the report was stolen by the Securitate informant code named Eugen Stanescu on February 26, 1964), DSS report dated July 1968, p. 515.
22. Ibid., p. 516.
23. Archives of CCRCP, Chancellery, File 15/1958.
24. Harrington and Courtney, *Tweaking the Nose of the Russians*, p. 147.
25. Khrushchev made two visits to Romania in June and August 1955. It is not clear during which visit Bodnaras approached him on this subject. See Nikita S. Khrushchev, *Khrushchev Remembers* (New York, 1970), pp. 513–514, and Sergiu Verona, *Military Occupation and Diplomacy: Soviet Troops in Romania, 1944–1958* (Durham, N.C., 1992), p. 83.
26. Verona, *Military Occupation and Diplomacy*, pp. 130, 132.
27. Harrington and Courtney, *Tweaking the Nose of the Russians*, p. 195.

28. Ibid., pp. 196–197.

29. *Cartea alba a securitatii*, vol. III, 1994, Report of the U.S. embassy in Bucharest dated February 26, 1964, p. 516.

30. Rosen, *Dangers*, p. 184.

31. *Cartea alba a securitatii*, vol. III, 1994, Report of the U.S. embassy in Bucharest dated February 26, 1964, p. 516.

32. *Romania-Israel, Documente diplomatice, 1948–1969*, p. 159

33. Shlomo Leibovici-Lais, letter to the author, April 13, 2003.

34. Rosen, *Dangers*, p. 188.

35. Ibid., p. 173; in July 1956, Rabbi Portugal met with American rabbis visiting Bucharest. This was held against him by the Securitate (see SRI archives, file 47240, vol. 1–3, RG 25.004M, reel 158). The father of the Transnistrian orphans was set free in August 1959 and a few months later allowed to emigrate to the United States.

36. Rosen, *Dangers*, p. 174.

37. Ibid., p. 188.

38. Ibid., p. 189.

39. Phone conversation with Shlomo Leibovici-Lais, May 11, 2003.

40. Rosen, *Dangers*, p. 189.

41. Harrington and Courtney, *Tweaking the Nose of the Russians*, p. 197.

42. Ibid.

43. Library of Congress, Romania, *Gheorghiu-Dej's Defiance of Khrushchev*, data as of July 1989.

44. Ibid.

45. Shlomo Leibovici-Lais, letter to the author, April 13, 2003.

46. Rosen, *Dangers*, p. 201.

47. *Romania-Israel, Documente diplomatice, 1948–1969*, pp. 163–166. The Israeli government wanted to send police inspector Abraham Sellinger to Romania and to other East European countries in order to find documents related to this investigation. The Romanian archives did indeed contain much material relating to the activities of Gustav Richter, Eichmann's envoy to Bucharest during World War II.

48. Harrington and Courtney, *Tweaking the Nose of the Russians*, p. 222.

49. Ibid., p. 224.

50. Romanian Ministry of Foreign Affairs Archives, Note 215/1964.

51. Harrington and Courtney, *Tweaking the Nose of the Russians*, p. 232.

52. Ibid., pp. 235–236; see also Gheorghe Gaston Marin, *In serviciul Romaniei lui Gheorghiu-Dej* (Bucharest, 1999), pp. 152–153.

53. Harrington and Courtney, *Tweaking the Nose of the Russians*, p. 258.

54. Deletant, *Ceausescu and the Securitate*, pp. 53–54.

55. Ibid., p. 66.

56. Ion Mihai Pacepa, *Mostenirea Kremlinului* (Bucharest, 1993), p. 405.

57. Deletant, *Ceausescu and the Securitate*, p. 209.

58. Ibid., pp. 208–209.

59. Stephen Bates, Pastor Richard Wurmbrand, "Cleric Driven by Missionary Zeal Despite Years of Persecution in Communist Romania," *The Guardian*, March 16, 2001.

60. Interview with Phyllis Yadin, London, March 16, 2002.

61. Ion Mihai Pacepa, *Red Horizons: Chronicles of a Communist Spy Chief* (New York, 1987), p. 74.

62. Ettinger, *Blind Jump*, interview with Shaike Dan, p. 345.

63. Ibid.

64. Ibid., pp. 345–347.

65. Pacepa, *Red Horizons*, p. 73.

66. Ibid., pp. 73–74.

67. Ibid., p. 74.

68. Ibid., pp. 74–75.

69. Pacepa, *Mostenirea Kremlinului*, p. 406.

5. AN UNEASY RELATIONSHIP

1. Pacepa, *Mostenirea Kremlinului*, pp. 253–254.

2. Ibid., pp. 255–256.

3. Craig R. Whitney, *Spy Trader: Germany's Devil Advocate and the Darkest Secrets of the Cold War* (New York, 1993); Christopher Andrew and Vasili Mitrokhin, *The Mitrokhin Archive: The KGB in Europe and the West* (London, 1999), p. 651.

4. Yosef Govrin, *Israeli-Romanian Relations at the End of the Ceausescu Era* (London, 2002), p. 262.

5. Deletant, *Ceausescu and the Securitate*, p. 210.

6. Govrin, *Israeli-Romanian Relations*, p. 262.

7. Interview with Liviu Turcu, August 19, 2003.

8. Pacepa, *Red Horizons*, p. 75.

9. Interview with Ion Mihai Pacepa, August 11, 2003.

10. Pacepa, *Red Horizons*, p. 75.

11. Ibid., p. 75.

12. Interview with an Israeli diplomat who requested anonymity.

13. Interview with Ion Mihai Pacepa, August 11, 2003.

14. Pacepa, *Red Horizons*, p. 75.

15. Ibid., pp. 75–76.

16. Tom Shachtman, *I Seek My Brethren: Ralph Goldman and "The Joint"* (New York, 2001), p. 184.

17. Interview with Cornel Burtica, Bucharest, March 23, 2002; see also Rodica Chelaru, *Culpe care nu se uita, Convorbiri cu Cornel Burtica* (Bucharest, 2001), p. 163.

18. Interview with Cornel Burtica, Bucharest, March 23, 2002.

19. Pacepa, *Red Horizons*, p. 75.

20. Interview with Cornel Burtica, Bucharest, March 23, 2002.

21. Interview with Liviu Turcu, August 19, 2003.

22. Document from a Romanian government archive that requested anonymity.

23. Romanian Ministry of Foreign Affairs Archives, nota de convorbire 05/03503 from April 14, 1970.

24. Tesu Solomovici, "Dosarul Sanmuel Francisc: povestea unui securist evreu trimis sa spioneze in Israel," *Ziua*, January 18, 2003.

25. Tesu Solomovici quotes as sources in his article two Israeli journalists, Yosi Melman and Eytan Haber, from the daily *Yediot Ahronot*.

26. Mihai Pelin, *DIE 1955–1980, Culisele spionajului romanesc* (Bucharest, 1997), p. 299.

27. Raviv and Melman, *Every Spy a Prince*, p. 235.

28. Rosen, *Dangers*, pp. 128, 221–222.

29. Ettinger, *Blind Jump*, p. 365.

30. Deletant, *Ceausescu and the Securitate*, pp. 103–105.

31. Pelin, *DIE 1955–1980, Culisele spionajului romanesc*, pp. 386–391.

32. Raviv and Melman, *Every Spy a Prince*, p. 225.

33. *Cartea alba a Securitatii*, vol. II, p. 562.

34. Govrin, *Israeli-Romanian Relations*, p. 253.

35. Deletant, *Ceausescu and the Securitate*, pp. 206–207.

36. Govrin, *Israeli-Romanian Relations*, p. 251.

37. Ibid., pp. 249–250.

38. Rosen, *Dangers*, p. 223.

39. Pelin, *DIE 1955–1980*, p. 368.

40. Information from a CNSAS/SIE file of a person who requested anonymity.

41. Radu Tudor, "Generalul Alexandru Tanasescu a murit in conditii suspecte," *Ziua*, January 21, 2003.

42. Library of Congress Country Studies, Area Handbook Series, Romania, "Emigration: Problem or Solution?" Data as of July 1989.

43. Pacepa, *Red Horizons*, p. 76.

44. Interview with Ion Mihai Pacepa, August 13, 2001.

45. Whitney, *Spy Trader*, p. 180.

46. Howard M. Sachar, *A History of Israel* (New York, 1976–1987), p. 661.

47. Calafeteanu and Cornescu-Coren, *Romania si criza din Orientul Mijlociu*, p. 51.

48. Preda, *Romania-Israel, Documente Diplomatice*, p. 259.

49. Calafeteanu and Cornescu-Coren, *Romania si criza din Orientul Mijlociu*, pp. 106–107.

50. Ibid., p. 124.

51. Ibid., p. 144.

52. Raviv and Melman, *Every Spy a Prince*, p. 235.

53. Pacepa, *Red Horizons*, p. 371.

54. Ettinger, *Blind Jump*, p. 353.

55. Raviv and Melman, *Every Spy a Prince*, p. 268.

56. Calafeteanu and Cornescu-Coren, *Romania si criza din Orientul Mijlociu*, p. 93.

57. Library of Congress Country Studies, Area Handbook Series, Romania, Middle East, Data as of July 1989.

58. Harrington and Courtney, *Tweaking the Nose of the Russians*, p. 292; Ceausescu's efforts to mediate between Washington and Beijing failed because China was suspicious of all East European Communist countries (see ibid., p. 296).

59. Christopher Andrew and Vasili Mitrokhin, *The Sword and the Shield: The Mitrokhin Archive and the Secret History of the KGB* (New York, 1999), p. 352.

60. Abba Gefen, *Israel at a Crossroads* (Jerusalem, 2001), p. 175.

61. Ettinger, *Blind Jump*, p. 355.

62. Sachar, *A History of Israel*, p. 732.

63. Preda, *Romania-Israel, Documente diplomatice*, p. 404.

64. Calafeteanu and Cornescu-Coren, *Romania si criza din Orientul Mijlociu*, pp. 94, 148–149.

65. Romanian Ministry of Foreign Affairs, cable from Bagdada, nr. 14.071 of April 27, 1970.

66. Calafeteanu and Cornescu-Coren, *Romania si criza din Orientul Mijlociu*, pp. 180–181, 185.

67. Ibid., p. 151.

68. Romanian Ministry of Foreign Affairs, fond 220–20, 1970.

69. Calafeteanu and Cornescu-Coren, *Romania si criza din Orientul Mijlociu*, pp. 99–100, 177.

70. Ibid., p. 162.

71. Ettinger, *Blind Jump*, pp. 353–354.

72. Ibid., p. 354.

73. Pacepa, *Red Horizons*, p. 95.

74. Ibid., p. 96.

75. Rosen, *Dangers*, p. 206.

76. Gefen, *Israel at a Crossroads*, pp. 162–163.

77. Ettinger, *Blind Jump*, p. 354.

78. Sachar, *A History of Israel*, p. 845.

79. Rosen, *Dangers*, p. 281.

80. Gefen, *Israel at a Crossroads*, p. 164.

81. Sachar, *A History of Israel*, p. 845.

82. Interview with Liviu Turcu, August 19, 2003.

83. Raviv and Melman, *Every Spy a Prince*, p. 226.

84. Ibid.

85. Ibid., p. 227.

86. Ibid., p. 228.

87. Ibid.

88. Ibid., pp. 235–236.

89. Mihai Pelin, *Din culisele spionajului romanesc, DIE 1955–1980*, pp. 145–146.

90. According to the June 7, 1993, agreement originating from a private Israeli archival source that requested anonymity.

91. Chelaru, *Culpe care nu se uita*, pp. 165–167.

92. Pacepa, *Red Horizons*, p. 425.

93. Ibid.

94. Interview with Liviu Turcu, August 19, 2003.

95. Ibid.

96. Pelin, *Din culisele spionajului romanesc*, p. 157.

97. Ibid., pp. 306, 387, 399.

98. Chelaru, *Culpe care nu se uita*, p. 208.

99. Deletant, *Ceausescu and the Securitate*, pp. 377, 381.

100. Interview with Liviu Turcu, August 19, 2003.

101. Nicolae Plesita, *Interview, Lumea Magazin*, nr. 11 (91), 2000. According to Plesita, who allegedly used information provided him by Chief Rabbi Moses Rosen, the Mossad was closing on Carlos when Ceausescu got cold feet and ordered CIE to severe all connections with the assassin. According to the author John Follain, the Securitate paid $400,000 to Carlos and "refused him nothing. A safe house in downtown Bucharest, sixty passports bearing false names (several of the passports were diplomatic), [and] three rocket launchers with eighteen projectiles and Romanian-made remote controls. He was even given a bank account in Bucharest, number 471 1210 3502, opened by Anna Luisa Kramer (alias Magdalena Kopp), Carlos' companion, at the Romanian Bank of Foreign Trade" (John Follain, *Jackal: The Complete Story of the Legendary Terrorist Carlos the Jackal* (New York, 1998, pp. 131–132). According to Mircea Raceanu, head of the U.S. desk at the Romanian Ministry of Foreign Affairs, early in October 1980, during a visit to Bucharest, the deputy secretary of state, Robert Berry, warned Stefan Andrei, the Romanian foreign minister, that the United States knew that the Romanian government had hired an Arab commando to liquidate Pacepa and that any attempts to implement this plan would have "serious consequences."

Berry asked Andrei to convey this message to Ceausescu. (Mircea Raceanu, *Infern 89* [Bucharest, 2000], p. 324.)

102. Gefen, *Israel at a Crossroads*, p. 177.

103. Dimitri Volgokanov, *Autopsy for an Empire: The Seven Leaders Who Built the Soviet Regime* (New York, 1988), p. 373.

104. Library of Congress Country Studies, Area Handbook Series, Romania, Middle East, Data as of July 1989.

105. Ibid.

106. According to the June 7, 1993, agreement originating from an Israeli private archival source which requested anonymity.

107. Ibid.

108. Ibid.

109. Govrin, *Israeli-Romanian Relations*, p. 137.

110. Ettinger, *Blind Jump*, pp. 376–377.

111. Govrin, *Israeli-Romanian Relations*, pp. 190–204; see also Library of Congress Country Studies, Area Handbook Series, Romania, Middle East, Data as of July 1989.

112. Library of Congress Country Studies, Area Handbook Series, Romania, Middle East, Data as of July 1989.

113. *Lumea Magazin*, Convorbire cu col. (r) Dumitru Burlan, "Eu am fost sosia lui Ceusescu."

114. Patrick Seale, *Abu Nidal: A Gun for Hire* (New York, 1992), p. 279.

115. Govrin, *Israeli-Romanian Relations*, pp. 140–142, 148, 151–153.

116. Library of Congress Country Studies, Area Handbook Series, Israel, Relations with Soviet Union. Data as of December 1988.

117. Library of Congress Country Studies, Area Handbook Series, Israel, Relations with Eastern Europe. Data as of December 1988.

118. Victor Ostrovsky, *The Other Side of Deception* (New York, 1994), p. 215.

119. Govrin, *Israeli-Romanian Relations*, p. 262.

120. Document from a Romanian government archive that requested anonymity dated August 20, 1988.

121. Document from a Romanian government archive that requested anonymity dated January 19, 1998.

6. THE MONEY TRAIL

1. Pacepa, *Red Horizons*, p. 72.

2. Ibid.

3. Library of Congress Country Studies, Area Handbook Series, Romania, Trading Partners, Data as of July 1989.

4. Ibid.

5. Library of Congress Country Studies, Area Handbook Series, Romania, Retirement of the Foreign Debt, Data as of July 1989.

6. Dennis Deletant, *Ceausescu and the Securitate*, p. 67.

7. Interview with Ion Mihai Pacepa, August 11, 2003.

8. Ion Mihai Pacepa in Sorin Rosca-Stanescu, *Autopsia: Demontarea unei inscenari securiste impotriva generalului Pacepa* (Bucharest, 1998), pp. 335–336.

9. Marius Oprea, Alya reflectat in arhivele securitatii, p. 8, Symposium, Diaspora Research Institute, Tel Aviv, December 2001. The document originates from the Archives of CCPCR/Comitetul Executiv nr 264/7/18/2/1972/Stenograme of the discussion with Alexandru Draghici, May 20, 1968.

10. Ibid.

11. Archives of the Romanian Ministry of Foreign Affairs, fond Israel, file 221/1961.

12. Ibid., file 220/1962; see also *Romania-Israel, Documente diplomatice, 1948–1969*, pp. 196–197.

13. Archives of the Romanian Ministry of Foreign Affairs, fond Israel, note 3770/3 IV, 1964.

14. Govrin, *Israeli-Romanian Relations*, p. 312.

15. Raviv and Melman, *Every Spy a Prince*, p. 235.

16. MAE Archives, cable from Tel Aviv, no. 71.314 from 24/IV/1969.

17. Pacepa, *Red Horizons*, p. 76.

18. Rosen, *Dangers*, p. 217.

19. Pacepa, *Red Horizons*, p. 75.

20. Interview with Phyllis Yadin, March 16, 2002; see also Pacepa, *Red Horizons*, p. 75; Mihai Pelin, *DIE, 1955–1980: Culisele spionajului romanesc* (Bucharest, 1997), p. 193.

21. Pacepa, *Red Horizons*, p. 73.

22. Mihai Pelin, *DIE, 1955–1980*, pp. 112–114.

23. Ibid., pp. 113–114.

24. Ibid., pp. 90, 114.

25. Pacepa, *Red Horizons*, pp. 71–73.

26. Interview with Ion Mihai Pacepa, August 11, 2003.

27. Dan Badea, *Averea presedintelui, Conturile Ceuseacu* (Bucharest, 1998), pp. 204–205.

28. Ibid.; the photocopy of the original document is reproduced in the appendix of Badea's book.

29. Interview with Ion Mihai Pacepa, August 11, 2003.

30. *Washington Post*, May 15, 1985, p. A1; see also Pacepa, *Red Horizons*, pp. 368–372.

31. Benjamin Weiser, "Ceausescu Family Sold Soviet Military Secrets to U.S.; Romanian Officials, Others in the East Bloc Arranged Arms Transfers," *Washington Post*, May 6, 1990.

32. Ibid.

33. Interview with Liviu Turcu, August 19, 2003.

34. Weiser, "Ceausescu Family Sold Soviet Military Secrets to U.S.," *Washington Post*, May 6, 1990.

35. Badea, *Averea Presedintelui*, p. 87.

36. Interview with Shlomo Leibovici-Lais, Tel Aviv, May 5, 2001.

37. Ettinger, *Blind Jump*, p. 353.

38. Library of Congress Country Studies, Area Handbook Series, Romania, Emigration: Problem or Solution? Data as of July 1989.

39. Ibid.

40. Library of Congress Country Studies, Area Handbook Series, Romania, Relations with Non-Communist States—West Germany. Data as of July 1989.

41. Library of Congress Country Studies, Area Handbook Series, Romania, Emigration: Problem or Solution? Data as of July 1989.

42. Whitney, *Spy Trader*, p. 182.

43. William Totok, "Romania anilor 70: o imagine nefardata, Memoriile unui fost ambasador la Bucuresti," *Observator Cultural*, Erwin Wickert, *Die glucklichen Augen. Geschichten aus meinem Leben*, Deutsche Verlagsanstalt (Stuttgart-Munchen, 2001).

44. Ibid.

45. Badea, *Averea Presedintelui*, p. 99.

46. Ibid., p. 88.

47. TV Documentary: "Evil's Fortune: The Fifth Estate," Linden McIntyre, Robert McAskill, Canadian Broadcasting Company, 1991; see also Badea, *Averea Presedintelui*, p. 96.

48. Interview with Ion Mihai Pacepa; see also Pacepa, *Red Horizons*, p. 76.

49. Badea, *Averea Presedintelui*, pp. 96, 97.

50. Ibid., p. 97.

51. "Evil's Fortune: The Fifth Estate."

52. Tom Shachtman, *I Seek My Brethren: Ralph Goldman and "The Joint"* (New York, 2001), p. 185.

53. Library of Congress Country Studies, Romania, Emigration: Problem or Solution? Data as of July 1989.

54. Document originating from a Romanian archive that requested anonymity.

55. Badea, *Averea Presedintelui*, p. 102, appendix.

56. Pacepa, *Red Horizons* (1990 edition), pp. 432–433.

57. Badea, *Averea Presedintelui*, p. 97; interview with Liviu Turcu, August 19, 2003; Jurnalul National, May 11, 2004.

7. THE WASHINGTON EQUATION

1. Library of Congress, Country Studies, Area Handbook Series, Romania–United States. Data as of July 1989.
2. David B. Funderburk, *Pinstripes and Reds: An American Ambassador Caught Between the State Department and the Romanian Communists, 1981–1985* (Washington, D.C., 1987), pp. 95–96.
3. Moses Rosen, "The Antisemitic Tyrant," *Revista Cultului Mozaic*, no. 685, February 1, 1990, p. 8.
4. Govrin, *Israeli-Romanian Relations*, p. 88.
5. Interview with Shlomo Leibovici-Lais, Tel Aviv, May 11, 2001.
6. Rosen, *Dangers*, p. 245.
7. Roger Kirk and Mircea Raceanu, *Romania versus the United States: Diplomacy of the Absurd, 1985–1989* (New York, 1994), p. 67.
8. Ibid., p. 5.
9. Ibid., prologue.
10. Govrin, *Israeli-Romanian Relations*, p. 88.
11. Library of Congress Country Studies, Area Handbook Series, Romania–United States. Data as of July 1989.
12. Harrington and Courtney, *Tweaking the Nose of the Russians*, p. 424.
13. Pacepa, *Red Horizons*, p. 275.
14. Nestor Rates to Radu Ioanid, April 15, 2002.
15. Rosen, *Dangers*, p. 246.
16. Rosca-Stanescu, *Autopsia*, pp. 107–108.
17. Harrington and Courtney, *Tweaking the Nose of the Russians*, p. 437.
18. Rosen, *Dangers*, p. 253.
19. Harrington and Courtney, *Tweaking the Nose of the Russians*, p. 425.
20. Funderburk, *Pinstripes and Reds*, p. 144.
21. *Romania: Human Rights in a "Most Favored Nation,"* June 1983, a report by the U.S. Helsinki Watch Committee.
22. Library of Congress Country Studies, Area Handbook Series, Romania, Emigration: Problem or Solution? Data as of July 1989.
23. Harrington and Courtney, *Tweaking the Nose of the Russians*, p. 502.
24. Library of Congress Country Studies, Area Handbook Series, Romania, Other Religions. Data as of July 1989.
25. Ibid.

26. Funderburk, *Reds and Pinstripes*, p. 90.

27. Rosen, "Antisemitic Tyrant," p. 8.

28. Harrington and Courtney, *Tweaking the Nose of the Russians*, p. 555.

29. Kirk and Raceanu, *Romania versus the United States*, p. 68.

30. Harrington and Courtney, *Tweaking the Nose of the Russians*, p. 626.

31. Ibid., p. 536.

32. Funderburk, *Pinstripes and Reds*, p. 34.

33. Kirk and Raceanu, *Romania versus the United States*, p. 14.

34. Library of Congress, Country Studies, Area Handbook Series, Romania–United States. Data as of July 1989.

35. Kirk and Raceanu, *Romania versus the United States*, p. 53.

36. Ibid., p. 57.

37. Ibid., p. 71.

38. Ibid., p. 275.

39. Ibid., p. 149.

40. Harrington and Courtney, *Tweaking the Nose of the Russians*, p. 574.

41. Kirk and Raceanu, *Romania versus the United States*, p. 173.

42. Ibid., p. 283.

43. Govrin, *Israeli-Romanian Relations*, p. 100.

44. Kirk and Raceanu, *Romania versus the United States*, p. 229.

45. Govrin, *Israeli-Romanian Relations*, p. 101.

46. Kirk and Raceanu, *Romania versus the United States*, p. 251.

47. Library of Congress, Country Studies, Area Handbook Series, Romania, Relations with West Germany. Data as of July 1989.

48. Mikhail Gorbachev, *Memoirs* (New York, 1996), p. 476.

49. Govrin, *Israeli-Romanian Relations*, p. 104.

50. Library of Congress, Country Studies, Area Handbook Series, Romania, The CSCE Meeting in Vienna. Data as of December 1988.

51. Kirk and Raceanu, *Romania versus the United States*, prologue.

8. "WHY DID YOU DRAIN MY SOUL?"

1. Ettinger, *Blind Jump*, p. 361.

2. Ibid., pp. 361–362.

3. Ibid., p. 379.

4. Interview, Shlomo Leibovici-Lais, May 11, 2001.

5. Gefen, *Israel at a Crossroads*, p. 166.

6. Sachar, *A History of Israel*, pp. 982–983.

7. Govrin, *Israeli-Romanian Relations*, p. 257.

8. Yossi Melman and Dan Raviv, "Buying Romania's Jews, How Israel Ransomed 120,000 People from Ceausescu," *Washington Post*, January 14, 1990, p. B5.

9. Black and Morris, *Israel's Secret Wars*, pp. 178–179.

10. Tad Szulc, *The Secret Alliance, The Extraordinary Story of the Rescue of the Jews Since World War II* (New York, 1991), pp. 286–287.

11. Ibid., p. 298; Black and Morris, *Israel's Secret Wars*, pp. 448–450.

12. Szulc, *Secret Alliance*, p. 305.

13. Document from an Israeli archival source that requested anonymity.

14. Jack Anderson and Dale Van Atta, "Ransom for Romania's Jews," *Washington Post*, October 20, 1991, p. C7.

15. Ibid.

16. Melman and Raviv, "Buying Romania's Jews."

17. Ettinger, *Blind Jump*, pp. 376–377.

18. Interview with Shlomo Leibovici-Lais, May 11, 2001.

19. Anderson and Van Atta, "Ransom for Romania's Jews."

20. Harrington and Courtney, *Tweaking the Nose of the Russians*, p. 606.

21. Michael McFaul, "The Russian Graduate," *Washington Post*, May 10, 2002, p. A37.

22. Harrington and Courtney, *Tweaking the Nose of the Russians*, pp. 610, 614.

23. Ibid., pp. 607, 615.

24. Melman and Raviv, "Buying Romania's Jews."

25. Pacepa, *Red Horizons*, p. 334.

26. Library of Congress Country Studies, Romania, Emigration: Problem or Solution? Data as of July 1989.

27. Interview with Ion Mihai Pacepa, August 11, 2003.

28. Silviu Curticeanu, *Marturia unei istorii traite* (Bucharest, 2000), pp. 96–97.

29. Ibid., p. 102.

30. Burtica in Rodica Chelaru, *Culpe care nu se uita*, pp. 89, 90, 215.

31. Govrin, *Israeli-Romanian Relations*, pp. 34–36.

32. Ibid., p. 67.

33. Weiser, "Ceausescu Family Sold Soviet Military Secrets to U.S."

34. Alexandru Barladeanu, *Despre Dej, Ceusescu si Iliescu, Convorbiri* (Bucharest, 1997), p. 233.

35. Interview with Shlomo Leibovici-Lais, May 11, 2001.

36. Marius Oprea, *Alya reflectat in arhivele securitatii*, Symposium, Diaspora Research Institute, Tel Aviv, December 2001, p.8.

37. Reuters, May 1, 1997.

38. Ibid.

Index

A NOTE ON THE AUTHOR

Radu Ioanid is director of international archival programs at the United States Holocaust Memorial Museum in Washington, D.C. Born in Bucharest, he was educated in Romania and in France, and now lives in Bethesda, Maryland. He has also written *The Holocaust in Romania* and wrote the Introduction to Mihail Sebastian's acclaimed *Journal 1935–1944*.

AMITYVILLE PUBLIC LIBRARY

3 5922 00194 0083

323.1192 Ioanid, Radu.

IOA   The ransom of the
          Jews.

$26.00

DATE			

AMITYVILLE PUBLIC LIBRARY
CORNER OAK & JOHN STS
AMITYVILLE NY 11701
(631) 264 – 0567

JUN 0 2 2005   BAKER & TAYLOR